THE
ESSENTIAL
GUIDE TO USING

Positive
Psychology

WITH CHILDREN
& YOUNG PEOPLE

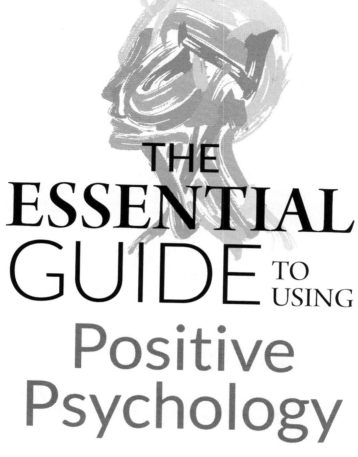

THE
ESSENTIAL
GUIDE TO USING

Positive
Psychology

WITH CHILDREN
& YOUNG PEOPLE

TINA RAE, HELENA BUNN & JODY WALSHE

HINTONHOUSE

First published in 2019 by

Hinton House Publishers Ltd
T +44 (0)1280 822557 F +44 (0)1280 822338
E info@hintonpublishers.co.uk

www.hintonpublishers.com

© 2019 Tina Rae, Helena Bunn & Jody Walshe

Reprinted in 2022

British Library Cataloguing in Publication Data
A CIP catalogue record for this book is available from the British Library.

ISBN 978 1 906531 84 3

Printed and bound in the United Kingdom

The Hinton House Essential Guides

*The Essential Guide to Using Mindfulness
with Children & Young People*

*The Essential Guide to Using Solution-Focused
Brief Therapy with Children & Young People*

*The Essential Guide to Using Cognitive Behavioural
Therapy (CBT) with Children & Young People*

*The Essential Guide to Using Positive Psychology
with Children & Young People*

The Hinton House Essential Guides are not intended to be used to deliver individual 'therapy' per se, but rather to contribute to the development of individual, small-group, or whole-class interventions, providing professionals with a series of tried-and-tested resources for use with young people. It is intended that they can be used not only to target those young people regarded as exhibiting behavioural problems, such as low self-esteem or anxiety, but that they may be used with all young people in order to prevent the escalation of any difficulties and to provide them with a range of therapeutic tools and problem-solving strategies and techniques to foster well-being and mental health.

The *Guides* are both educational and therapeutic in design, but are not, in any sense, a substitute for individualised interventions delivered by appropriate clinicians. However, the resources can and do provide useful tools for the clinician engaged in such individual interventions and the school-based Learning Mentor/ SENCO/Inclusion Manager wishing to develop a programme of support for an individual student or groups of students in the school context and beyond.

These practical and user-friendly guides are intended to provide a useful introduction to each approach or intervention, whilst also empowering professionals to safely make use of appropriate tools and strategies to foster emotional and psychological well-being.

Contents

Activities & Resources

Activities

Activities for Children

Activities for Adolescents

About the Authors

Dr Tina Rae

Consultant Psychologist Compass Fostering
Author and educational consultant
tinarae@hotmail.co.uk

Dr Tina Rae has more thirty years' experience working with children, adults and families in both clinical and educational contexts within local authorities and specialist educational services. She currently works as a consultant educational and child psychologist in a range of SEMH and mainstream contexts and for Compass Fostering as a consultant psychologist supporting foster carers, social workers and looked-after children. From 2010 to 2016 she was an academic and professional tutor for the Doctorate in Educational and Child Psychology at the University of East London. Tina is a registered member of the Health and Care Professions Council and a full member of the British Psychological Society. She is also a member of ENSEC (European Network for Social and Emotional Competence) and a former trustee of the Nurture Group Network (NGN) now NurtureUK.

Tina has published more than 100 titles on topics including well-being, attachment, emotional literacy, behavioural problems, anger and stress management, critical incidents, cognitive behavioural therapy, motivational interviewing, solution-focused brief therapy, loss and bereavement in young people, youth offending and social skills development.

Among her most recent publications are *The Essential Guide to Using CBT with Children & Young People* (2018), *Identifying & Supporting Children with Sensory Processing Difficulties* (2018), *Understanding & Preventing Self-Harm in Schools* (2107), *The Essential Guide to Using Mindfulness with Children & Young People* (2017), all from Hinton House Publishers.

Tina is a regular speaker at both national and international conferences and events and also provides training courses and supervision for school-based staff in both special and mainstream contexts and educational psychology services across the UK and internationally.

Dr Helena Bunn

Dr Helena Bunn graduated in Psychology from the University of Bucharest, Romania, before moving to England and completing a three-year Professional Doctorate Programme in Educational and Child Psychology at the University of East London.

In Romania Helena worked as a psychologist in education, whilst taking on roles as part-time university tutor, then lecturer, assistant director and, lastly, director at a Romanian university. During the 1990s Helena co-designed and delivered a range of inclusion training programmes to schools and has published work in this field. She became involved in international activities with Germany, Israel and Finland, focused on learning and sharing experience in the areas of special educational needs practices and support systems for specific groups of disadvantaged children (immigrant and publicly fostered).

On coming to England in 2004, Helena continued working in similar areas, after re-qualifying as a practitioner psychologist in education. She is currently a senior educational psychologist within Norfolk Local Authority, Educational Psychology and Specialist Support services, and an academic and professional tutor (principal lecturer) at the University of East London. She also provides expert evidence in Special Educational Needs and Disability Tribunal and Family Court cases.

Helena has undertaken research and has published material (both within the UK and abroad) in areas relevant to educational psychology practice, including special educational needs, inclusion, children with complex medical conditions and looked-after children. Her current research interests include making a positive difference in children's lives, and the role of children, parents and schools in this aspect. She has taught courses in aspects of child development, research methodology, special educational needs, psychological assessment and organisational change.

The passion guiding Helena's work has been, and remains, to search for and identify the 'diamond in the rough' in every individual, but especially in children: to help the individual shine by inviting and co-constructing impactful stories and then to amplify those stories to individuals and to others, and promote the process of positive change.

Dr Jody Walshe

Dr Jody Walshe is an educational and child psychologist. She completed her Doctorate in Educational and Child Psychology at the University of East London. Jody is also a consultant psychologist providing consultations for foster carers and supervising social workers with the Compass Community as part of their REACH approach. She is a registered member of the Health and Care Professions Council.

Before commencing her training in Educational Psychology, Jody worked as a teacher, learning-support assistant and tutor with young people aged between 5 and 19 years. The focus of much of her work looked at anxiety and mental health issues in school settings.

Jody has undertaken research on self-harm in school settings, including the experiences and training needs of school staff. Her work focuses on a wide range of areas including: techniques to support the emotional development of children and young people; staff resilience and well-being; self-harm, self-esteem, anxiety, eating disorders and bereavement; attachment in the classroom; and staying safe online.

Jody has co-authored *Understanding and Preventing Self-Harm in Schools: Effective Strategies for Identifying Risk & Providing Support* (2017) with Tina Rae, *The Essential Guide to Using Mindfulness with Children & Young People* (2017) with Tina Rae and Jo Wood, and *The Essential Guide to Using Solution Focused Brief Therapy (SFBT) with Children & Young People* (2018) with Tina Rae and Miles Thomas, all from Hinton House Publishers.

A note about this book

It is important to be aware that this is not a therapeutic approach;
however, it introduces the whole concept of Positive Psychology
and the need to support children in recognising and developing
their own strengths. As a result, the introduction covers the key
concepts and ideas of Positive Psychology in some depth and we
would recommend that you make yourself aware of the primary
tools and philosophy behind this approach.

Introduction

During recent years there has been a great deal of research that highlights the inextricable link between an individual's well-being and their capacity to achieve. Exploration into the cycles of thinking, feeling and behaving, and relating that enable us to succeed both socially and academically remains ongoing.

The link between education and happiness has become firmly established as mutually reinforcing: education helps individuals to be happy and happy people gain more from education. Research undertaken by Positive Psychologist Barbara Frederikson (2009) confirms the idea that children and young people who present as happy and content in the school and social contexts will generally perform better in academic and life skills development. These are the students who develop social and emotional competency, a growth mind-set and the creativity, grit and energy needed to succeed in all areas of their lives.

The focus in this *Essential Guide* is to therefore present the practitioner with a succinct background to the development of Positive Psychology and the ways that it can be applied in the learning context through the range of school systems. Key resources are alluded to and some explained in slightly more depth so as to enable the practitioner to support students in developing their strengths and engaging more positively in both the learning and social contexts.

1 Positive Psychology at a Glance

Positive psychology is a relatively new field, but many centuries ago the Greek philosopher Aristotle (384–322 BCE) was already preoccupied with 'what it means to live a good life'. This fascination was shared by later psychologists, including Abraham Maslow (1943), who was particularly interested in human growth and even used the term 'positive psychology'. More recently, Rogers (1961) initiated the 'humanistic' movement in psychology, which is primarily interested in the 'growth' of a human being; humanistic psychologists approach the study of human beings from a fresh, strength-focused and optimistic perspective.

Whilst positive psychology established clearly that it aims to catalyse change from a medical model of deficit or disease to building positive qualities (Seligman & Csikszentmihalyi, 2000), it does not intend to replace this medical model, but rather focuses on a previously neglected component in psychology (Seligman et al., 2002).

A recurring theme of this new science is that using our strengths taps into the core of who we are as human beings, and that it is through these that we can make our greatest contribution. Jenny Fox Eades (2008), Programme Director for Schools and Young People at the not-for-profit Centre for Applied Positive Psychology explains that Positive Psychology studies areas like contentment, hope, optimism, pleasure and engagement. It focuses on positive traits such as love, courage and creativity and virtues like citizenship, tolerance and responsibility.

Widespread Attention & its Dangers

At the beginning of the last decade very few people had heard of the term 'positive psychology', but now its effects can be felt across the nation. For most of us here in the UK, the biggest visible effect has been a stream of headlines and features devoted to this new science. Positive Psychology has proved itself much more media-friendly than traditional psychology and its study of weakness, pathology and mental illness. From BBC programmes investigating the happiness quotient of entire towns (such as the television documentary in 2004, *Making Slough Happy*) to parliamentary groups investigating the nation's well-being, we are gradually beginning to embrace the idea that we can master our positive emotions, and recognise success not just by what we earn, what we do, or where we live, but by our feelings of satisfaction and authenticity.

Maybe because of its huge popularity, Positive Psychology means different things to different people. Take, for instance, a participant in a Positive Psychology conference: when asked what Positive Psychology means, she replies: 'Oh, positive psychology. Yes, we could do with some of this!'

It is important to underline that Positive Psychology studies people whose lives are happy or fulfilled, in order to learn from them and to help others achieve this state of happiness. It has scientific foundations and its thinking is based on a number of studies: it is not simply the focus on positive thinking and positive emotions. In his latest book *Flourish; A visionary new understanding of happiness and well-being and how to achieve them*, Martin Seligman (2011) explains that he has now come to detest the 'H word', a term which he considers has now been so overused that it has become almost meaningless. He challenges the generally accepted view that Positive Psychology is primarily about seeking happiness and suggests that we have lost contact with the spiritual and philosophical traditions of happiness and have settled for a weaker, more selfish version, which is about enjoyment, pleasure and the avoidance of pain and suffering.

What is Happiness & Well–Being?

What makes for a satisfactory or worthwhile life? Every culture shares ideas of a worthy life. As we will describe later in the book, this means that an individual's beliefs about the 'good life' are influenced by the shared understanding that circulates within their community. These beliefs are organised, moreover, to respond to fundamental human needs and also to potentially fulfil the individual as a human being.

Happiness is seen as both subjective and objective. In their exploration of happiness, Seligman & Royzman (2003) describe three stages of happiness in life:

1 **Pleasant Life** – a life that successfully pursues positive emotions about the present, past, and future. This stage is realised when we appreciate experiences to do with friends or a partner, the natural environment, and our bodily needs. Examples of us these experiences would be eating food that we like, doing activities that we enjoy (such as shopping or attending a football match), having time off with friends, going on vacations, having a house, and generally having as many pleasures as possible. Generally people in the Western societies may experience this stage and some may persist indulging in it.

2 **Good Life** – another stage of achieving happiness, which focuses on discovering our unique virtues and strengths and employing them creatively to develop our lives. People in this stage have a balanced focus on the main areas of life, involving work or education, play and love. In the 'good life' we experience happiness when we achieve competence and when we discover and use our strengths to reach a positive state of energy and enjoyment when engaged – this state of enjoyment is also described as the *flow* state.

3 **Meaningful Life** – The last stage of happiness, in which we find a deep sense of fulfilment by employing our unique strengths for a purpose greater than ourselves.

In *Flourish* Seligman (2011) revisits this model and explains how 'flourishing', rather than happiness, has become a more appropriate term to describe this state of well-being. Flourishing is defined as 'a state of positive mental health: to thrive, to prosper and to fare well in endeavours free of mental illness, filled with emotional vitality and function positively in private and social realms' (Michalec *et al.*, 2009, p.319).

Indeed, existing figures show that only 18 per cent of adults meet the criteria of flourishing: 65 per cent are moderately mentally healthy and 17 per cent are languishing. Unsurprisingly, flourishing has several positive correlates, such as academic achievement, mastering the skill of goal-setting, higher levels of self-control and continued perseverance (Howell, 2009). Thus, a science that focuses on the development and facilitation of flourishing environments and individuals is an important addition to the psychological sciences.

PERMA — a New Model of Psychological Well–Being & Happiness

As discussed earlier, Positive Psychology has proved popular, both with the general public and amongst the scientists. This has favoured its development and, although its history is short, it has evolved rapidly, backed by a vast amount of research. Several models for understanding human happiness have, consequently, developed. One of the most influential is PERMA, a revised model of well-being devised by Seligman in 2011 (here 'well-being' is understood as subjective happiness or fulfilment). In his revised thinking, Seligman (2011) advises that there are five elements that can help people reach a life of fulfilment, happiness, and meaning:

1 **P**ositive emotion
2 **E**ngagement
3 **R**elationships
4 **M**eaning
5 **A**ccomplishment

PERMA's elements

Positive emotion This has one of the most obvious connections to happiness and it is about viewing past, present and future experiences in a positive and optimistic way. Here it is important to understand that positive emotion is related to enjoyment, rather than pleasure. Whilst pleasure is about satisfying bodily needs for survival (e.g., thirst, hunger, sleep), enjoyment comes from intellectual stimulation and creativity: for example, when a child completes a challenging task, such as building a Lego car with sustained concentration, or solving a difficult mathematical problem, they will be beaming with joy and satisfaction from their work. This type of positive emotion is essential, as when someone enjoys the tasks in their lives they are more likely to persevere and face challenges by finding creative and alternative solutions.

Engagement   This is usually known as 'flow' and refers to the well-being one experiences when totally absorbed in the task in hand, so much so that one loses track of time and feels at one with what is being done. It is, of course, a given that everyone is different and we all find enjoyment in different things, such as exercising, dancing, working on projects, or on the same task. This element is important as it stretches our intelligence, skills, and emotional capabilities; in doing this we learn, grow and nurture our personal happiness.

Relationships   It is well established that we are social animals who thrive for connection, love and strong and meaningful interactions with other people. Interestingly, research shows that our brain activates pain centres when we are at risk of becoming isolated. Building positive relationships has a contagious effect and, in turn, offers us support in difficult times.

Meaning   We experience a sense that life has meaning when serving a cause bigger than ourselves, which in turn gives us a subjective feeling of well-being. Interestingly, research shows that meaningful activities are more strongly related to well-being than the pleasurable ones. Maybe this explains why most adults chose to have children than not to have them, despite the well-known fact that childless couples have a greater sense of happiness than those with children. That said, having children may feed the sense of meaning in one's life and consequently offer a greater well-being than not having children. Paradoxically, whilst parents are less happy than childless families, they also experience greater well-being! Leaving aside building a family, people might seek meaning by practising a religion, or committing time to charitable actions and political causes.

Accomplishment   Whilst we were taught that 'winning isn't everything', we do need to win sometimes. What would our goals and plans be if we never reached them? This element is, therefore, about us having a sense of accomplishment – this happens when we look back at our experiences and life and say, 'Yes I did it, and

I did it well!' This element is important, because creating and working towards goals helps us anticipate and build hope for the future. Past successes make us feel more confident and optimistic about future attempts. When we feel good about ourselves, we share our wisdom of success more readily with others. We will maintain our motivation and strive to continue to achieve. We may even become role models for those around us!

PERMA's applications

The PERMA model can be applied to every aspect of our life, including personal development, group work, and other settings, and can help people develop new cognitive and emotional tools.

At a very general level, being aware of the PERMA model is the first step in our journey. By referring back to its elements we can start attempting to apply the model to aspects of our life. Getting a positive perspective, finding the things that make us happy and can make us fully engaged are some of the first steps towards our comfort, happiness and well-being. Focusing on your relationships with your family and friends by finding ways to connect and enjoy others' company is the next step, whilst finding the meaning to our lives and what gives us a sense of purpose is a highly individual and subjective experience.

2 Positive Psychology & Education

⌒ᴑ

Whilst the movement of Positive Psychology continued to develop and mature, appetite for its application in education also commenced. Two of the first advocates for Positive Psychology in education were Huebner and Hills, who looked at existing research and made the case for Positive Psychology practices in schools. In their article 'Does the Positive Psychology Movement have Legs for Children in Schools?' (Huebner & Hills, 2011), they criticise the limited practical value of the current widespread practice of using a deficit model when identifying individuals with poor school adjustment. They bring into discussion a number of findings, including Suldo and Shaffer's (2008) dual-factor model of mental health and conclude that, by including positive measures when investigating mental health, the resulting picture would serve as a more comprehensive lens through which to understand, predict and promote optimal outcomes for children in education.

Whilst accepting that Positive Psychology still needs to prove its usefulness in education, Huebner and Hills (2011) point to the existing studies as offering a strong scientific foundation for the use of Positive Psychology with children.

On a general level, Positive Psychology is beneficial in schools because it encourages individuals to strive to do their best; disapproval, on the other hand, has been shown to have the opposite effect. It might be useful to remind the reader of an old study made by Dr Elizabeth Hurlock in 1925, in the course of which students were praised, criticised or ignored, based on specific work at school. The students who were praised recorded the greatest improvement of 71 per cent; those criticised improved by 19 per cent, whereas the pupils provided with no feedback improved by a mere 5 per cent. Although later studies have looked more specifically into the power of feedback, it is obvious that praise seems an effective method of fostering improvement.

Positive Education

Positive education is a relatively recent approach, which brings up the application of Positive Psychology in educational contexts and aims to incorporate the five elements of well-being from PERMA model (discussed in previous chapter) into the life and work of schools. In his book *Flourish*, Seligman (2011) defines Positive Education as traditional education focused on academic skill development, complimented by approaches that nurture well-being and promote good mental health and writes that 'higher human accomplishment is one of the four components of flourishing and yet another reason that will and character are indispensable objects of the science of positive psychology' (p.125).

The point that many educators are missing, suggests Seligman (2011), is that schools need not be obsessed with exams to be successful. The 'exam factory' mentality is robbing teachers of their professionalism and pupils of curiosity and delight in learning. Seligman writes that if we want to maximise the achievement of children, we need to promote self-discipline, which he describes as 'the queen of all the virtues, the strength that enables the rest of the strengths'.

Positive education incorporates the PERMA model, to which it adds the concept of character strength. Whilst not intending to detail the framework of the positive education model, which is available in other papers, we will be focusing on features of Positive Psychology used in positive education that have been proved to work.

Developing Positive Habits

Increasing our well-being is inextricably linked to cultivating the right habits. There are a number of activities that have been studied in relation to the influence on how we feel. Feeling positive emotions and engaging in positive relationships are two of the activities that are positively related to our well-being. Mindfulness and compassion are other activities that are shown to support our growth.

The positive emotion

Experiencing positive emotions enables us to develop a better understanding of our emotions and those of others, as well as a greater ability to initiate, practise, lengthen, and create further positive emotions in our lives. Barbara Fredrickson (2009) found that a positive outlook on life not only widens our prospects, but also keeps us vigilant to opportunities that we otherwise would not have noticed. Experiencing positive emotions – and hence being positive in our outlook – also helps us cope with difficulties, as we are more ready to look for and find opportunities that we would not have seen before, which leads to even more positive emotions.

Interestingly, Clifton and Anderson(2002) consider positive emotions an essential daily requirement for survival and found that ninety nine out of one hundred people prefer the influence of positive people, as they believe that they work more productively when they are around positive people.

Positive emotions are contagious and, even more, they can contribute to an upward spiral (see above, 'Social Contagion), which means that being more positive and optimistic makes us more open to do and see things that will lead us to achieve the things we want in life. At school, having a teacher or student who is positive can help the other students to be positive and work to the best of their abilities.

Positive relationships

Enjoying the company of our peers, being positive and supportive, devoting time to develop relationships, and surrounding ourselves with people who make us feel good are all important factors in our lives. Friends and family help give meaning to our lives, fulfil our need to belong, and provide support during tough times. Boosting our positive relationships helps us to get involved in activities through understanding the nature of engagement, the pathways to it, and the impact it has on individual well-being.

A positive education involves healthy, caring and supportive interpersonal relationships with others. Roy Baumeister (2005, p.109) summarises the evidence: 'whether someone has a network of good relationships or is alone in the world is a much stronger predictor of happiness than any other objective predictor'.

Martin Seligman (2011, p.80) suggests that all too often schools emphasise critical thinking and following orders rather than creative thinking and learning new material, with the result that many children 'rank the appeal of going to school just slightly above going to the dentist'. 'In the modern world', writes Seligman, 'I believe that we have finally arrived at an era in which more creative thinking, less rote following of orders and, yes – even more enjoyment will succeed better.'

Our schools are places that give children the tools that they will need to design their futures. Rather than simply preparing our children and young people for lives of security and self-sufficiency, we should also encourage developing a sense of hope and the ability to be resilient in the face of uncertainty. Optimism, collaboration, creativity, emotional intelligence and motivation are also resources that will support our young people to grow into strong and self-determined adults.

Character Strength

What is the character?

Tough (2012, p.20) writes that the character is one of those words that 'can complicate any conversation because it can mean different things to different people'. Although the character ordinarily relates to traits, or qualities, which are distinctive to an individual and are built into an individual's life, hence assuming some degree of autonomy and stability, Peterson and Seligman (2004) propose a definition of the character, as a set of abilities or strengths that are very much *changeable*. They imply that the character contains skills that we can learn and practise, and moreover, can be taught. Further, Peterson and Seligman's approach does not focus on external values, such as morality and ethics, but on personal growth and achievement.

Building a strength–focused approach & universal virtues

Character strengths are capacities or ways of thinking, feeling and behaving that are morally valued. According to a strength-focused approach, each individual has unique qualities that can be used to enhance well-being, overcome challenges, and nurture relationships.

Christopher Peterson and Martin Seligman (2004) standardised the concepts of virtue and strengths. They looked across 3,000 years of cultures and religions and identified what they considered were the core virtues that can be found in all of them. Faced with hundreds of character strengths they applied several criteria in order to distil the key strengths that they believed to be universal. This process resulted in the identification of six universal virtues: wisdom, courage, humanity, justice, temperance and transcendence. We achieve these virtues through our own strengths of character. Twenty-four strengths were defined and accepted as the strengths that allow us to achieve these virtues. The 24 character strengths, organised into the six universal virtues, are listed below.

1 **Wisdom & Knowledge.** Strengths that are all about learning and using new knowledge:

- *Creativity.* Thinking of new ways of thinking and acting
- *Curiosity.* Exploring; taking an interest in what is going on in the world and wanting to find out about new things
- *Open-mindedness/judgement.* Seeing things objectively and fairly, from all sides; thinking things through carefully before making up your mind; weighing up all the evidence; being able to change your mind when you get new information
- *Love of learning.* Constantly developing skills and knowledge and enjoying finding out more about the things that you already know
- *Perspective.* Being wise and looking at the world in a way that makes sense, being able to give others good advice

2 Courage. Emotional strengths and being able to overcome difficulties and reach one's goal:

- ↻ *Bravery.* Not shrinking from threat, challenge, difficulty, or pain; speaking up for what is right; acting on convictions, even if unpopular

- ↻ *Persistence/perseverance.* Finishing what you start, keeping going even if things are difficult; enjoying finishing tasks

- ↻ *Integrity.* Presenting oneself in a genuine way; taking responsibility for one's feeling and actions

- ↻ *Vitality.* A zest and enthusiasm for life and living; taking responsibility for your feelings and actions and not blaming somebody else when things go wrong

3 Love. Interpersonal strengths; looking out for and being a friend to others:

- ↻ *Intimacy.* Enjoying being close to people, valuing, sharing and caring for others

- ↻ *Kindness.* Doing things for others without requiring reciprocation

- ↻ *Social intelligence.* Being aware of how yourself and others are motivated; knowing how to fit in and behave in lots of different situations

4 Justice. Dealing fairly with people:

- ↻ *Teamwork.* Being socially responsible and loyal; working well as a member of a team and doing your share

- ↻ *Fairness.* Treating everyone in a similar way; being just and without bias

- ↻ *Leadership.* Encouraging your team or group to get things done; organising activities and making sure that they happen

5 Temperance. Not overdoing things:

- ↻ *Forgiveness and mercy.* Forgiving those who have done wrong; giving people a second chance

- ↻ *Humility/modesty.* Not putting oneself above others; letting achievements speak for themselves

- ↻ *Prudence.* Making careful choices; not taking big risks; not saying or doing things that you will later regret

↪ *Self-control.* Controlling one's emotions and actions according to one's values

6 Transcendence. Strengths that make connections to the universe and provide meaning in life:

↪ *Wonder.* Noticing and appreciating beauty and excellence

↪ *Gratitude.* Being aware of and thankful for the good things that happen to you; taking time to say thank you

↪ *Hope.* Expecting the best in the future and working towards it; believing that a good future is something that can be built

↪ *Humour.* Enjoying laughter and making people laugh; seeing the lighter side of life

↪ *Spirituality.* Having beliefs about the meaning of the universe and about life that shape one's behaviour and provide comfort

Adapted from Peterson & Seligman,
Character Strengths & Virtues, 2004

Chris Peterson and Martin Seligman created a tool for measuring the above character strengths – called the Values in Action Inventory of Strengths (VIA-IS). This is deemed to be a practical tool for 'diagnosing' strengths. It is a cross-cultural tool and a number of studies, also undertaken in the UK, have proven its universality across cultures.

Peterson and Seligman believed that cultivating these strengths represented a reliable path to the 'good life' (p.640), a life that is not just happy, but also meaningful and fulfilling. Character strengths can function as a substitute for the social safety net (i.e., the support from their families, and culture and ease, which individuals from supportive backgrounds have, and which protects them from the negative consequences of social detours, mistakes and bad decisions).

This means that if a person does not benefit from the safety net that comes from a supportive background, that person will need more grit, social intelligence and self-control. Developing these strengths takes a great amount of time and effort; nonetheless, when acquired, these strengths act as protective factors for individuals, and Peterson and Seligman believe that they could provide the compensation that an individual requires in order to succeed.

Strengths are important pathways to 'flourishing'. Students who use their strengths have been found to demonstrate strong academic performance, which supports the idea that these are invaluable in student accomplishment.

The power of rules

Whilst improving our ability to delay gratification is related to building positive (hybrid) habits, Jennifer Fox Eades (2008, p.219) also suggests that we can exercise our self-control like a muscle. This means that we can train our ability to delay gratification, just as we can train our muscles in the gym. The essence of being successful in training this mental 'muscle' is to promise some small reward – and then to deliver this reward over and over again, until our brain says: 1) 'Yes, it was worth the wait'; and 2) 'Yes, I have the capability to do this'.

When we achieve this stage, it means that we have assimilated a new rule that will serve as a mental habit; this, in turn, will reduce the amount of energy we will have to spend on delaying gratification in the specific area that we have targeted as important.

Jennifer Fox Eades explains that the reasons why 'the rules' work is because they enlist the prefrontal cortex as your ally against the more reflexive, appetite-driven parts of your brain. Rules are not the same as will-power. They are a meta-cognitive substitute for will-power. By making yourself a rule you are bypassing the painful, internal conflict involved in exercising your determination to resist a treat. Rules provide structure, because they prepare us for encounters with temptations and enable us to redirect our attention elsewhere.

Building Resilience

In recent years, resilience has gained a great deal of attention – both in the academic arena and in some areas of social media.

The term appears to have become part of what we, as educators and those caring for children and young people, feel is a part of our role in supporting children's development – to increase levels of resilience and thus build overall levels of well-being.

However, fear that the term 'resilience' will become a cliché can limit the power the word has in our classrooms and in the social, emotional and academic development of our students. Resilience has a place in our schools and, ultimately, in the lives of our students, and *building resilience through key tools of Positive Psychology is something that all of us can develop as part of our practice.*

Resilience is a skill that cannot be overlooked. In fact, it can be a skill that is the difference between surviving and *thriving*. For students living in poverty, students who have barriers to learning, or students experiencing stress and trauma, it may be the skill that makes *all* the difference.

Educators and those in the caring professions are essential facilitators of resilience skills development. We have the unique opportunity to influence the social and emotional growth of our students beyond the scope of the academic curriculum. In a time when everything appears to be so readily available to us, experiencing struggle or awaiting an answer can be a lost art. Teaching students the skill of resilience and providing them with opportunities to bounce back and renew themselves in the face of adversity becomes a fundamental necessity. Schools are successful when they provide students with skill sets that will allow them be successful both behaviourally and academically.

Even though resilience is an internal experience, there are things we can do to help students tap into and build their skills. The following are five guiding strategies that propel resilience development forward and concurrently improve behaviour and academic performance. These can be deployed at both a whole-school and classroom level.

1 **Show them their purpose & know yours.** For many students, having an adult that cares about and believes in their strengths and abilities is irreplaceable and we know that teacher effectiveness is a better determinant of student performance than race, socio-economic status, or class size. The influence of these key adults is palpable and should be recognised in all that they do to support their students. But students also need to recognise, understand and value their place in the larger context. Providing learning opportunities which include supporting and caring for others, offering choices in the classroom, and assigning students roles and jobs relevant to their interests and talents all establish purpose and make students feel like a necessary spoke in the wheel.

2 **Allow students to experience success & struggle.** Success comes in various forms. Allowing students to realise their strengths elevates their confidence and their belief in their own potential. This, of course, also requires us to recognise and incorporate students' different learning styles and to tap into students' diverse intelligences in all areas of the curriculum. Alongside this, it is also essential that we highlight and continually reinforce the importance and value of struggle and failure. We need to move students away from the notion that failure is bad and something to be avoided. Providing specific feedback, focusing on mastery versus completion, and having students identify what they learned from their mistakes establishes a culture of resilience – that is, a culture of 'trying again', and 'I can't do it – yet!', whenever possible.

3 **Set high expectations.** Setting high expectations for students lays the groundwork for possibilities. When students know that those around them believe in them, they tap into this notion every time they encounter a challenge. We know that without this belief, resilience is not possible. Because when there is failure – and inevitably there will be – they are more apt to move beyond their doubts to reach success. In situations where students are presented with many challenges, it can become too easy for them, and even their teachers, to be overwhelmed by the obstacles. It is therefore imperative at this point to overcome sympathy or defeat and move to empathy and optimism. It is important to keep expectations high and end destinations in view, whilst still respecting the diversity of our students and offering alternative routes or ways of achieving their goals.

4 **Create a supportive environment.** Neither students nor teachers have the power to change the conditions under which students live. What teachers do have power over is creating the educational conditions for these students to succeed *despite* the adverse circumstances in which they may live. Cultivating a school environment in which students are safe and successful is the foundation of resilience development. Students need to feel comfortable and safe in their classrooms – and comfortable and safe in admitting failure or seeking assistance. Environments where students are encouraged to take risks and be individuals allow for freedom to be actualised. If schools do not provide students with this environment, students are limited by their perception of the definition of success. Schools that believe in the growth mind-set – that is, that students are a gold mine of untapped potential – ultimately allow for resilient learners to be nurtured. The five essential feelings that are crucial to an individual's emotional well-being (competence, belonging, usefulness, potency and optimism) need to be fostered at both the whole school and individual level.

5 **Promote self-advocacy & communication.** An ultimate goal for all of those working with children and young people should be to support the development of essential life skills. Employing problem-solving skills, navigating the norms of social behaviour, and communicating needs are just a few of the vital skills that will allow students to bounce back from life's struggles in adult life. Having these self-advocacy skills will provide students with the ability to overcome obstacles and identify what they need in order to move forward.

School–Based Approaches

In general, the literature surrounding Positive Psychology-based interventions is abundant and varied and it seems that interventions may have different effects on different groups of people. Dawood, for instance, in his recent article about school-based positive psychological intervention (2013), finds that females are more open to being involved in such interventions and hence benefit in more ways from interventions than do males. He also identifies that younger children are rarely involved in Positive Psychology interventions that are specific to well-being.

One of the ways that Positive Psychology could be applied in school is as a universal intervention, at whole-school level, as this helps foster the success of all students in an educational setting and enhance their lives by not only minimising harmful symptoms, but also by raising the overall baseline of happiness.

Overall, what is important is that the practitioner adopts the approaches that clearly have the best evidence base. According to Wilson (2011) strengths-based interventions can have lasting effects, as it is clearly motivating for young people to have their strengths identified and acknowledged and to subsequently ensure that the resulting behaviours become self-sustaining. Individuals can adopt a new behaviour that, in turn, prompts a revision of their self-image. For example, 'I must be the sort of person who really cares about others'. The key to this approach is that individuals develop a more positive view of themselves that build on and reinforces itself leading to sustained change. This is the approach that we would advocate as psychologists working directly and indirectly with children and young people in the learning context.

Positive Psychology & Positive Thinking

We support the premise that working from a strengths-based perspective is more motivating for both students and practitioners than addressing weakness and deficits. Within education this is particularly pertinent and useful. Positive Psychology as a movement and set of interventions has experienced evident growth since its formal appearance two decades ago. This may well be due to the optimistic name of this perspective, its focus on personal growth rather than on deficit and the ease with which we can understand the key concepts. Positive Psychology now has huge popularity, which nonetheless also comes with some problems. One of the most common mistakes that people make is to consider positive psychology to be the same thing as positive thinking.

It is therefore important to understand that there are several differences between positive psychology and positive thinking, including:

- Positive thinking highlights positivity in all situations, whereas Positive Psychology offers a variety of tools for success.

- Although presented in accessible language and concepts, it is important to recognise the strong evidence base for Positive Psychology's approach and also to highlight the fact that it makes use of information and research from studies of depression, anxiety or other mental health problems.

- Positive thinking could be loosely termed as optimism, which is helpful in a variety of situations. On the other hand, Positive Psychology believes that, at times, a realistic or even negative view of a situation could be more helpful. There is a healthy ratio of positives to negatives: there are times when it is just not appropriate to plaster a smile on your face.

So, ultimately, this is the rationale for adopting these approaches and ensuring that young people have the opportunity to thrive in both the learning and social contexts.

We next include a range of pertinent and useful activities that we have found to be effective at a range of levels in the school context in order to both introduce and develop an understanding and use of Positive Psychology.

3 How to Use this Essential Guide

The first part of the *Essential Guide* describes the most important elements of Positive Psychology and is intended to provide an easily understood theoretical background that can be shared with children, young people and the adults working with them.

In the second part, you will find some key activities that we have found most helpful with children and young people at both an individual and group level. They are self-explanatory and relatively straightforward to follow and implement. Many are worksheets or information sheets that the young person can complete during the session, or keep for future use to stimulate their thoughts about the topic or the activity.

The activities are not intended to provide a comprehensive intervention, but we have included those that we have found to be most useful when working directly with our own students.

1 The activities are divided into those designed for children (Chapter 4), adolescents (Chapter 5) and groups (Chapter 6).

2 Any of the activities may be adapted for use with individuals, small groups, or whole classes, as appropriate. There is some overlap between the chapters and you are encouraged to try out and adapt activities from different chapters once you are familiar with the principles of the Positive Psychology-based approach and the needs of your children/young people.

3 The activities have been designed with maximum flexibility in mind: they stand on their own, or may be mixed and matched according to individual/group interests, needs and motivations.

4 The Resources section includes an information sheet and consent form for parents and a 'Top Tips' sheet for teens. These handouts should be useful as you begin your planned programme of Positive Psychology sessions.

Before You Start

It is suggested that you consider the following key ideas before you start working with an individual or group:

- **Information.** The child/young person needs to understand what kind of things they will be doing and why. They will need time and space to ask questions and have concerns answered.

- **Consent.** Informed consent should be sought from the children and young people who will be taking part in the sessions, and from their parents/carers. See the Resources section at the end of the book for an information sheet and sample consent letter.

- **Motivation.** The child/young person needs to want to engage in the activities and the process, or at least to have some curiosity or interest.

- **Containment and relationship.** The child/young person needs to feel supported and emotionally contained by the facilitator before they begin to engage in learning and activities. Think about: introductions, ground rules, non-verbal communication, group size, creating a secure, fun and trusting atmosphere, in which everyone's ideas matter.

- **Individual differences.** Before starting work, think about the young people you are going to be working with and try to identify any important factors that should inform your planning, for example: language skills, Special Educational Needs, learning style, and so on. All of the tools and activities included can be adapted to suit the child's language ability and development.

- **Environment.** Try to find a private, calm space that you work in each time.

- **Time.** Think about using a timer to maintain structure and pace your sessions.

- **Feedback.** Ask how it went afterwards; listen to this feedback and act on it.

↪ **Record and reflect.** Think about noting down very briefly any reflections or action points for your next session, so as to extend your learning as well as that of your group.

↪ **Practise! Practise! Practise!** Integrating positive psychology strategies and practice into the regular school routine will help it to become part of the culture of the classroom. Finding a regular time (e.g., when the children have come back into the classroom after lunch or at the start of the school day) will help with this.

↪ **Back Up.** Consider in every session how to encourage generalisation of the skills learnt beyond the immediate session, for example: using take-away tasks, diaries, communication across the school and with home, inviting visitors to the positive psychology sessions , and so on.

Activities

∽

Activities for Children

Activities for Adolescents

Activities for Groups

4 Activities for Children

4.1 Well-being & Me

4.2 Positive Postcards

4.3 Hero Stories

4.4 Happy Memories

4.5 I'm Grateful for...

4.6 Thank You Letter

4.7 Kindness

4.8 Being a Kindness Hero

4.9 When Someone Was Kind to Me

4.10 Three Good Things

4.11 Do More

4.12 My Future

4.13 Climb The Mountain

4.14 What is a Habit?

4.15 Happiness Log

4.16 My Happiness Shield

4.17 My Positive Scroll

4.18 Happy Habits to Relieve Uncomfortable Feelings

4.19 Recording My Uniqueness – This is Me!

4.20 Message in a Bottle

Activity 4.1
Well-being & Me

Aims

To discuss what well-being means and to think about how it applies to our own lives.

Activity

Begin by discussing what well-being means. Key points to cover:

- Feeling good

- Having energy

- Getting on with our friends

- Getting on with our family

- Knowing our strengths/what we are good at

- Doing our best

- Feeling as if we can cope with little problems

- Liking ourselves

- Feeling proud of ourselves

- Enjoying life

Ask the child to label the outline of the body on Worksheet 1 with some of the key words that the child thinks are important. Invite the child to be as creative as possible with different coloured pens/pencils.

Discuss the words they are choosing and why they think that they are important.

Worksheet 4.1
Well-being & Me

Write the well-being words that YOU think are important for YOU!

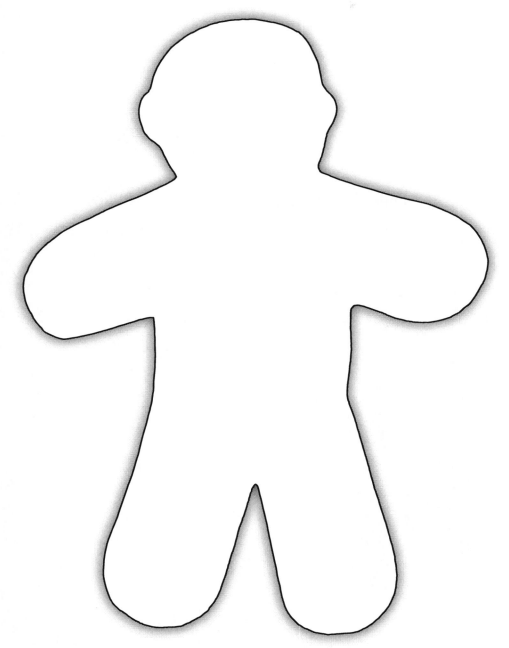

Activity 4.2
Positive Postcards

Notes

Ask the child to create two postcards to send to someone they care about. Using Worksheet 4.2, they can draw a picture of themselves doing something that is good for their well-being. Encourage them to decorate their cards in any way they like; you may wish to provide other 'stick-on' decorations, such as stars, and so on.

Then ask the child to write down on each postcard how these positive activities make them feel; this enquiry into how they *feel* when they are doing something reinforces understanding of why the activity promotes well-being.

Worksheet 4.2
Positive Postcards

Imagine you are sending postcards to someone special. Draw pictures for two Positive Postcards in the boxes below. Each postcard needs to show you doing something that helps your well-being.

Then use the blank lines below your picture postcard to tell your special person what you are doing and how it makes you feel.

Postcard 1

What I am doing _____

_____

When I do this it makes me feel _____

_____

_____

Postcard 2

What I am doing _____

_____

When I do this it makes me feel _____

_____

_____

Activity 4.3
Hero Stories

Notes

Choose a favourite story or short book that features a heroic character. Read the story with the child and ask them to reflect on it by answering the following questions:

1 Who was the hero in this story?

2 Why were they a 'hero'?

3 What challenge or dilemma did the hero overcome?

4 What personal strengths did the hero possess?

5 What choices did they have to make?

6 How did other people support the hero?

7 What did the hero learn?

8 How do we use the same personal strengths when we overcome obstacles in our own lives?

9 Can you share some examples?

To round off the session, the child may want to write their own heroic story or draw a picture of the heroic character you have discussed and write down that character's strengths.

Activity 4.4
Happy Memories

Notes

This activity helps the child to remember happy memories. It is important to support the child to understand that happy memories are an important part of maintaining well-being.

Begin by introducing the child to the idea that they may find it helpful to think about happy memories when they are finding something tough: lots of people do this and find it helpful.

Then, using Worksheet 3, ask the child to draw or write about their happy memories. This is an activity during which the child is invited to be as creative as they like, using a range of drawings, pictures, or other materials.

Worksheet 4.4
Happy Memories

Create your Happy Memories Picture in the frame below and include events, people and objects!

My Happy Memories

Activity 4.5
I'm Grateful for ...

Notes

Begin by explaining that everyone has things to be grateful for in their lives. Thinking about these things and expressing our gratitude makes us feel even luckier and will increase our sense of well-being.

Using Worksheet 4.5, invite the child to write or draw things in their life for which they are grateful.

Ask them if writing or drawing these things – thinking about them and giving them 'attention' – actually makes them feel happier? Suggest that this is perhaps an activity they might try every day.

Worksheet 4.5
I'm Grateful for ...

Thinking about the things we are GRATEFUL for means thinking about the things we feel LUCKY to have. Remembering them makes us feel good.

Think of all the things you are grateful for. Perhaps you feel grateful for someone in your family, your pets, home, school, toys, special friends, nature all around you?

Write all the things you feel grateful for in the four shapes below.

Activity 4.6
Thank You Letter

Notes

This activity builds on Activity 4.5, 'I'm Grateful for ...' and continues to deepen the child's understanding that gratitude is a positive.

Ask the child to write a letter to someone thanking them for something that the child feels lucky to have in their life. Spend some time discussing:

↪ Who they have chosen to thank

↪ Why they wish to thank them

↪ What they want to say

If the child does decide to give the letter to the person, be sure to follow through in a later session with two key questions:

↪ How did your letter make the person feel?

↪ How did giving the letter to the person make you feel?

Activity 4.7
Kindness

Start the session by discussing kindness and how it makes us feel. Things to discuss include:

- What is kindness?

- When someone is kind to us, how does it make us feel?

- How does the person who has been kind feel?

- Is there someone who has been particularly kind to you?

- What did this person do?

- How did you feel?

- Who are the 'kindness heroes' in your life?

Then ask the child to complete Worksheet 4.7, a written record of their 'kindness heroes'.

Worksheet 4.7
Kindness

Being kind makes us feel good!

Who are your kindness heroes? They might be from your life, or books or films.

My Kindness Heroes are _____

★ _____
_____
_____

★ _____
_____
_____

★ _____
_____
_____

★ _____
_____

Activity 4.8
Being a Kindness Hero

Notes

Continue the discussion begun in Activity 4.7, 'Kindness', but encourage the child to think of a time recently when they were kind to someone else.

☞ Have you ever been a 'kindness hero' for someone else?

☞ What did you do?

☞ What did that person say to you?

☞ How did it make you feel?

Ask the child to use the discussion and their own reflections to complete Worksheet 4.8.

Worksheet 4.8
Being a Kindness Hero

Think about a time when you were kind to someone

Draw it or write about it here.

How did it feel to you when you were kind to someone else?

_____

_____

_____

Activity 4.9
When Someone was Kind to Me

Notes

Continue the discussion begun in Activity 4.7, 'Kindness', but encourage the child to think of a time recently when someone was kind to them.

✍ Think about a person who has recently been kind to you.

✍ What did that person do?

✍ How did it make you feel?

Ask the child to use the discussion and their own reflections to complete Worksheet 4.9.

Worksheet 4.9
When Someone Was Kind to Me

Think about a time when someone was kind to you.

Draw it or write about it here.

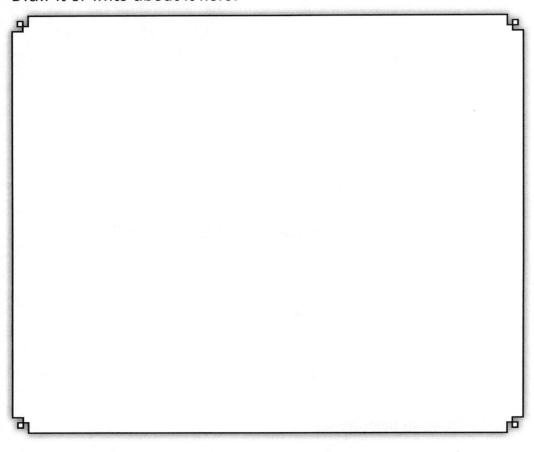

How did it feel when that person was kind to you?

_____

_____

_____

Activity 4.10
Three Good Things

Notes

This session builds on Activity 4.5, 'I'm Grateful for ...', and Activity 4.6, 'Thank You Letter'. The focus is on taking time to be grateful for good things, because having a sense of thankfulness and appreciation is very important to well-being. We know that people who are grateful tend to be happier, healthier and more fulfilled. It can sound strange, but being grateful can also help people to cope with stress. You may want to ask the child why they think it is important to be grateful. You may want to ask them how they felt when they did the 'What I'm Grateful for ...' and 'Thank You Letter' activities.

Introduce these ideas and emphasise that even on bad days there are good things that we can see and it is helpful to notice them, even if they are small.

This activity also provides a structure for helping children to recognise that noticing positives can help them to rise to challenges, rather than dwelling on negatives.

This activity has two worksheets. Worksheet 4.10a simply asks children to identify three good things: they may want to write them down or draw them. Worksheet 4.10b is slightly more complicated, as it also includes a 'why' section for each good thing, to help the child

page 1 of 2

to see *why* each good thing makes them feel good/positive/grateful. You may feel a child would benefit from starting off with Worksheet 4.10a and then building up to using Worksheet 4.10b after a few sessions. Other children would be ready to start with Worksheet 4.10b in the first session, and you can support them to think about *why* something has made them feel good.

Some children will require support to engage in this activity and you can help them to think about everyday examples of 'good things', for instance:

- I sat next to my friend at lunch.

- We had a PE lesson.

- I am reading a book I like.

- I played football at lunchtime.

In the session you will help them to practise using the two worksheets by thinking about three good things that happened yesterday. You may want to use the school timetable to help the child to remember the day and what they did and what might have been good.

Once the child has completed this activity with you, provide them with seven additional copies of each worksheet so that they can try to use these to record their 'good things' on a daily basis for a week. Ask them to bring the completed worksheets along to your next session.

How did the child feel about this activity?

Worksheet 4.10a
Three Good Things 1

Each day write down three good things that happened. They can be anything you feel good about or grateful for.

To get used to the idea, start by filling in the boxes below to describe three good things that happened to you **yesterday** and why they were good.

Good Thing 1
Good Thing 2
Good Thing 3

Now repeat this activity **at the end of each day** for a week. Use the seven blank copies of this worksheet that you have been given to write down your Three Good Things each day.

Worksheet 4.10b
Three Good Things 2

Each day write down three good things that happened. They can be anything you feel good about or grateful for.

Start by filling in the boxes below to describe three good things that happened to you **yesterday** and why they were good.

This time, try to include **why** you felt each of the things was really good.

Good Thing 1

Why ...

Good Thing 2

Why ...

Good Thing 3

Why ...

Now repeat this activity **at the end of each day** for a week. Use the seven blank copies of this worksheet that you have been given to write down your Three Good Things each day.

Activity 4.11
Do More

This is another opportunity for the child to reflect on the positive things they do every day and to try and increase these – and therefore transform their life in positive ways. Discuss the following points:

- How do you know if an action in your life is positive?

- What sort of actions do you already take that make you feel good in your daily life?

- Are there more positive actions that you would like to add to your list of positive things you do every day?

- What steps can you take to start adding these positive actions to your life?

- Why is this important?

- What would the results be in your life if you added more daily positive actions?

After discussion and reflection, ask the child to complete Worksheet 10.

Worksheet 4.11
Change Your Behaviour & Change Your Life!

Think of things you would like to do MORE often!

Write or draw them in the frame below

THINGS I WANT TO DO MORE OFTEN!

Activity 4.12
My Future

Notes

Discuss the effect that having dreams, hopes and ambitions may have on our feelings about everyday life. You could ask the following questions:

☞ Think of some dreams and hopes that you have for your future.

☞ When you think about these, how does it make you feel?

☞ Do you think that having dreams and hopes plays a role in your happiness?

☞ What would life be like if you had no dreams and hopes?

☞ How would you feel?

☞ Is it important to think that we can make our dreams and hopes come true?

☞ How does it feel if you dream about something that you know cannot come true?

☞ How important is it to make a practical plan for achieving our goals?

☞ Can we ask for help in reaching our goals?

☞ What kind of help would be useful?

After discussion and reflection, first ask the child to write down a list of their main dreams and hopes. Then, using this list, they can complete Worksheet 4.12, which asks them to focus on the practical steps they could take and the help they might get to achieve their goals.

Worksheet 4.12
My Future

MY FUTURE

These are the things I am going to do to make my dreams and hopes for the future come true ... write them down, or draw them on a separate sheet of paper.

1 _____

_____

2 _____

_____

3 _____

_____

4 _____

_____

These are the things I would like other people to do to help me to make my dreams and ambitions for the future come true ...

1 _____

_____

2 _____

_____

3 _____

_____

4 _____

_____

Activity 4.13
Climb the Mountain

Notes

This activity builds on Activity 4.12, 'My Future', in supporting the child as they learn to plan and persevere when working towards their goals. They will also begin to experience, practically, the benefit of small successes in boosting their emotional well-being.

You may want to leave the child to continue with the tasks they have set for themselves, but plan several follow-up sessions to see how they are progressing and to offer support.

Start with a discussion that raises the following questions:

☞ How important is it to our happiness to set ourselves small goals?

☞ Is it important to our happiness to feel ourselves achieving our goals?

☞ Can we make practical plans to achieve them?

☞ How will you feel if you achieve tiny successes every day or week?

☞ If you achieve success in small ways, how does that affect how you feel about tackling more difficult tasks?

☞ Think of a dream you have and ask yourself if you can see three or four little steps that you can take towards achieving it.

Now ask the child to complete Worksheet 4.13. You may wish to use glue to stick the tasks and goals to the mountain side. Some children standing 'at the foot' of their mountain, will need more support and encouragement than others. Appropriate follow-up sessions will offer this support.

Worksheet 4.13
Climb the Mountain

Write or draw all your goals/things you would like to do on a piece of paper. Cut them out and then arrange them on the mountain below. Place the ones that seem easiest to achieve at the bottom, the most difficult at the top and the slightly easier ones in the middle.

NEXT – start with the first and easiest task – when you've achieved it, climb a little further up the mountain and try the next one. Remember – take SMALL steps to reach the TOP!

Hardest

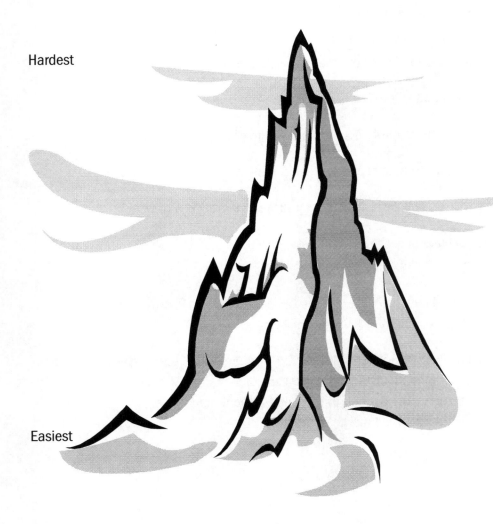

Easiest

Activity 4.14
What is a Habit?

Notes

Discuss what a habit is, and how people can have both 'good' and 'bad' habits.

☞ Think about habits we have that are good and others that might be bad habits.

☞ Discuss how our habits can affect our lives and also our overall well-being.

Ask the child to use the discussion and their own reflections to complete Worksheet 4.14.

Discuss with others in the group and see if there is any agreement on what is a good habit and what is a bad one.

☞ Do you think that some of our habits can help us to become happier people?

☞ What is a happy habit?

☞ What things do you do on a daily basis that make you experience more positive feelings?

Worksheet 4.14
What is a Habit?

Think about the different habits that people can have, and how some might be good and some might be bad habits.

Us the form to make two lists, one of habits that you think are good and one of habits you consider to be bad.

Do you think that some of our habits can help us to become happier people? What is a happy habit? What things do you do on a daily basis that make you experience more positive feelings?

Good Habits	Bad Habits

Activity 4.15
Happiness Log

Notes

Discuss how we can feel different levels of happiness at different times of day, depending on what we are doing or what is happening to and around us.

Using Worksheet 4.15, ask each child to keep a record for one day of what they are doing at different times, and when they feel happy or when they have made other people happy.

Worksheet 4.15
Happiness Log

For one day, keep a daily happiness log.

Record your activities and moments when you felt happy or made others happy.

	What I Did	How I or Others Felt
7.00am		
8.00am		
9.00am		
10.00am		
11.00am		
12.00 noon		
1.00pm		
2.00pm		
3.00pm		
4.00pm		
5.00pm		
6.00pm		
7.00pm		
8.00pm		
9.00pm		

Activity 4.16
My Happiness Shield

Notes

Think about and discuss the different sorts of things that make us feel happy and which can stop us feeling stressed and unhappy in difficult situations. These can be:

- Objects

- Other people

- Thoughts

- Feelings

- Behaviours

These can form our Happiness Shield. If we visualise this shield and all that it means, at difficult times or when we are feeling stressed, we can recall and use these strengths.

Using the shield outline on Worksheet 4.16, ask each child to write or draw the things they can do, think or feel to feel happy.

Worksheet 4.16
My Happiness Shield

On the shield, write or draw all the things, people, thoughts, feelings and behaviours that make you happy and give you strength to cope with any difficulties you might face.

You can use your shield at difficult times and visualise it giving you protection.

Practice this happy habit!

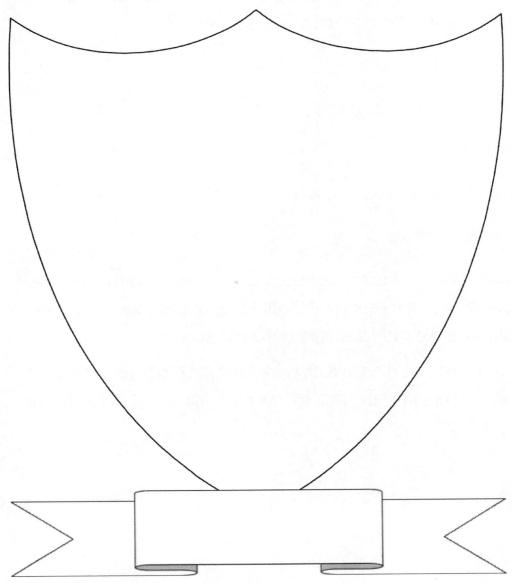

Activity 4.17
My Positive Scroll

Notes

Think about and discuss the different sorts of things that make us feel happy and which can stop us feeling stressed and unhappy in difficult situations. These can be:

- Objects

- Other people

- Thoughts

- Feelings

- Behaviours

These can form our Happiness Shield. If we remember some of these things at difficult times or when we are feeling stressed, they can help us to stay happy.

Using the shield outline on Worksheet 4.16, ask each child to write or draw the things they can do, think or feel to feel happy.

Worksheet 4.17
My Positive Scroll

Sometimes we forget to think about the positive or good things that happen – this is **not good**!

Every evening, think of one thing (at least!) that has happened during the day that made you feel good. Record these times on your Positive Scroll. At the end of the week **look** at the list – now you'll know that positive things really do happen to you!

Activity 4.18
Happy Habits to Relieve Uncomfortable Feelings

Notes

There are many different strategies that we can use to help us feel more happy and to help us relax when times are difficult or when we feel uncomfortable.

Using Worksheet 4.18, look at and discuss the suggestions – which ones might work best and in which situations? How could we turn these into a habit?

Ask the child to think of their own strategy – is there something they already do, or might start to do to help them feel happy?

Worksheet 4.18
Happy Habits to Relieve Uncomfortable Feelings

✍ Consider each of the strategies below.

✍ Tick the ones that you think you might be able to use.

✍ When do you think each strategy might help you most?

✍ Is there something you could do that is not listed here?

PHYSICAL EXERCISE A good walk, run or swim can help you to get rid of angry or anxious feelings. ☐ Yes ☐ No	**CONTROLLED BREATHING** Slowly breath in, hold for 5-10 seconds and then slowly let out the breath. As you do this, say 'RELAX' to yourself. ☐ Yes ☐ No
CALMING PICTURES Visualise a special place in your mind – somewhere really restful and peaceful. Turn this picture on when you feel uncomfortable. ☐ Yes ☐ No	**READING** Read a book – escape into a fantasy world to relax. ☐ Yes ☐ No
LISTENING TO MUSIC Listen to your favourite music – something that makes you feel happy and relaxed and takes your mind off the problem. ☐ Yes ☐ No	**Think of your own ... what works for you apart from these?**

Activity 4.19
Recording My Uniqueness – This is Me!

Notes

Discuss how everyone is different and how every person is has different qualities and is good at different things.

Ask everyone to think about all the different things that they like about themselves, and write or draw these in the spaces provided on Worksheet 4.19.

Worksheet 4.19
Recording My Uniqueness — This is Me!

I like myself because...

I like myself because...

I like myself because...

I like myself because...

Accept & Respect Yourself

I like myself because...

I like myself because...

I like myself because...

I like myself because...

Signed _____   Date _____

Activity 4.20
Message in a Bottle

Notes

Ask everyone to come up with a special message to place in a bottle and send to a friend who might be having difficulty overcoming a problem.

On the note, the child can describe how they have developed an ability to help with their own difficulties and how they would like to share this in order to help their friend.

Worksheet 4.20
Message in a Bottle

Write a note to a friend to support them in developing their skills and abilities.

☞ Tell them about how you have developed a talent or an ability and how you have overcome problems by developing a skill that you were previously bad at doing.

☞ Explain that you would like to support them in overcoming their own problems.

☞ Send the message to your friend!

SEND THE MESSAGE IN THE BOTTLE

5 Activities for Adolescents

Activity 5.1
Building Strengths

These are the 24 character strengths. Look at each one. Try to formulate a definition for each; you can look up words to help you. What does each strength mean to you?

1 Creativity

2 Curiosity

3 Open-mindedness

4 Love of learning

5 Keeping perspective

6 Bravery

7 Persistence

8 Integrity

9 Vitality

10 Love

11 Kindness

12 Social Intelligence

13 Citizenship

14 Fairness

15 Leadership

16 Forgiveness

17 Humility

18 Prudence

19 Self-Regulation

20 Appreciation of Beauty

21 Gratitude

22 Hope

23 Humour

24 Spirituality

> **Now you have come up with your own definitions ...**
>
> Put the strengths in order: first those that are your greatest strengths, then your weakest. Now reflect upon these in more depth.
>
> How can you further build upon your greatest strengths?
>
> Where/in which situations might you be able to use them in the future?

Activity 5.2
Investigating Strengths

Notes

This activity can be used as a stand-alone activity, or it can be used to follow on from Activity 5.1, 'Building Strengths'. This activity provides a structure for the young person to assess their strengths and then focus on using these in new ways.

Worksheet 5.2
Investigating Strengths

Step 1: Identify your strengths

Carry out the VIA Character Strengths assessment here (takes up to 30 minutes):

www.authentichappiness.sas.upenn.edu/Tests/SameAnswers

The assessment is called 'VIA Strength Survey for Children'. You will need to set up a log-in to use this site.

This shows which of 24 character strengths are your 'signature strengths'. Make sure you answer the questions on the assessment as you really are, not how you think you should be!

How do these results compare to your earlier assessment? What has changed?

Note down your **top five strengths** from the survey results:

Strength 1
Strength 2
Strength 3
Strength 4
Strength 5

Step 2: Review your strengths

Have a look at each of your top 5 in turn and ask yourself:

🖙 Do you feel naturally drawn to this strength (excited, energised, etc.)?

🖙 Do I feel surprised by it – is this the real me?

🖙 How much do I use this strength currently (at work, at home, etc.)?

🖙 Would others see it in me? (If you're not sure, ask them!)

If you don't feel that one of the five is the real you, then look at numbers 6, 7 or 8 and ask the same questions. Get to a list of 5 that you feel really are 'you'.

Step 3: Use your strengths

Pick one of your top 5 strengths and ask yourself:

🖙 How do I use this already and in what areas of my life?

🖙 What are other areas in my life that I could use it more?

🖙 What are other ways I could use it?

Every day over the next week, try to use this strength in a new way or a new area of your life.

Repeat the following week, using another of your top 5. And so on ...

Based on work by Seligman M.E., Steen T.A., Park N. & Peterson C. (2005)

Activity 5.3
The Meaning of Happiness

Notes

This is an activity that asks the young person to think about what happiness really means. The activity involves answering a series of questions.

Worksheet 5.3
The Meaning of Happiness Questions

1 How important are these factors in being happy?

    Money

    Having power

    Being young

    Being important or famous

    Good health

    Interesting work

    Good friends

    Love

    Having a flashy car, a nice house

    Having children

2 Does happiness depend on factors like these? Or does it depend on a person's attitude to life and other people?

3 Does happiness come to us by accident? In what ways can we make ourselves happy? Some people who are seriously ill appear to be happy all the time. How is that possible? Is it better not to think about being happy or unhappy?

4 What are the things in your daily life that constantly make you happy? How could you be happier than you are now?

5   Are these important factors in unhappiness?

      ↻ Being without love

      ↻ Having nothing to do

      ↻ Being ill

      ↻ Being lonely

      ↻ Hurting someone else

6   Who is the happiest person you know? Why are they happy?

7   Is it possible to be happy without other people? Would you be happy if you lived alone in a forest or desert? What can a lonely person, for example someone who has lost their partner through death or divorce, do to make their life happy?

8   Are men and women happy in different ways and for different reasons?

9   Why do some people have a feeling of guilt when they are very happy? Is it wrong or selfish to be happy?

10   Is it important to be happy?

Activity 5.4
My Happiness

Take a moment to think about what happiness **means** to you. Record whatever comes into your head.

> **What does happiness mean to you?**

Now think about specific things that often make you happy. These could be activities, people, places or anything else that comes to mind.

> **What things make you happy?**

Share this with someone else in the group and discuss.

Activity 5.5
Positive Diary

To help you to focus on **all the evidence** in your current situation, rather than just challenging or threatening problems and worrying thoughts or images, start to keep a Positive Daily Diary.

This is a brief note – on paper, your phone, tablet or computer – of anything you notice each day that appears 'positive': enriching, pleasing, a reminder of nature, happy, warm, loving, and so on ...

For example:

Monday	I watched a blackbird building a nest in the tree outside my bedroom window.
	My friend at school asked how I was doing.
	My head teacher told me I had done a good job.
Tuesday	The shop assistant complimented me on my manners.
	I smiled and said 'hello' to my elderly neighbour.
	I noticed how fluffy the clouds looked.
Wednesday	I had a message from my granny that cheered me up.
	I stopped and admired some flowers.
	I went for a short run and felt better.
	My friend sent me a text that told me she loved me.

✐ Practice keeping your diary on a daily basis – it may only take up 5 minutes of your time to write down what you've noticed.

✐ Review your diary once per day to remind yourself of what you have recorded.

✐ Notice what impact this has on your mood, thoughts, behaviour.

Activity 5.6
What I Overcame & What I Learned

Notes

As a teacher or learning professional, share a personal story about a time you had to work hard to get better at something. In this story, highlight:

↪ Hard work

↪ Strategies

↪ Help from others

Here's an example below of a personal story to share with students:

When I was in Year 5, I remember struggling with adding negative numbers. I had a hard time understanding what a 'negative' even meant when talking about a number — how can you have less than nothing? I ended up going through many of the sums in the maths text book and continuing to get many of them wrong.

I was very shy when I was a child so I didn't ask my teacher many questions, as I just did not have the confidence to do that. My thought was that I had reached the 'peak' of my ability in maths, and that it was basically all going to be downhill from here.

I eventually asked my mum about this topic and she explained to me the basic concept of negative numbers. This helped me understand it a little, but it was still unclear to me. I then researched on the internet for some examples from real life to show what these mysterious numbers represented outside of some abstract universe. Some of them made sense and others didn't. I still didn't entirely get it and I was so anxious that I

page 1 of 2

wanted to just give up (or continue hoping that negative numbers were not going to appear in my maths lessons ever again).

I started to dislike the subject simply because I couldn't understand it anymore. However, instead of entirely giving up, I eventually gathered the courage to ask my teacher for help as well. She explained it in a few different ways and gave me new strategies to try out. After some practise with these new strategies, I started to solidify my understanding of negatives, which allowed me to quickly pick up basic algebra afterwards. While it was a lot of hard work and I wanted to give up at many points during my journey, I eventually was able to 'rewire' my brain so that negative numbers actually made sense to me.

Ask the student to share a story about a time that they made their brain smarter.

Discuss the story and what they have learned from it. Consider the key themes: working hard, taking on challenges, and finding the right strategy can make people smarter.

Activity 5.7
A Letter to a Future Student

This activity involves asking the young person to write a letter about a learning-related struggle that they have experienced.

Ask the young person about a struggle they had when they were learning.

☞ How did it make them feel?

☞ How did they overcome it?

☞ What did it teach them?

Tell them to write a letter to a future student to tell them about their struggle, what they learned from it, and any advice they could give to the other student.

Save the letter in order to give it back to the young person during difficult, testing periods, such as final exams.

Additional activity

This activity looks at neuroplasticity and builds on the work done in the 'letter' activity.

Ask the young person to create a poster, painting, video, PowerPoint presentation or simple computer programme to show how the brain works.

Ask them to answer these questions:

☞ What is neuroplasticity and how does it work?

☞ What are neurons? How can they change over time? How do we know this?

☞ What are ways of making your brain grow?

☞ What is a growth mind-set?

Encourage the young person to be creative and scientific when explaining how learning can help develop the brain. If possible, allow them to research for themselves.

If working with a group or whole class, display these projects around your room or in the school corridors and refer to them throughout the year to motivate and offer a friendly reminder of the brain's plasticity.

Activity 5.8
Setting My Goals

My Friendship Goal

My Education Goal

My Career Goal

My Leisure Goal

My Health Goal

My Priority Goal is:

Think about your Priority Goal and ask yourself:

1 On a scale of 1 to 10 how much good will come if you achieve this goal and everything turns out well?

2 On a scale of 1 to 10 how much will your life be affected if you don't achieve this goal or things do not turn out well?

Think about it:

↪ If your answer to 1 is bigger than your answer to 2 it is clear you should go for it.

↪ If your answer to 2 is bigger than your answer to 1, think about a different goal.

↪ If your answers to 1 and 2 are the same, think about how you can increase the upside. Then just do it.

↪ If you can't think of an upside, don't do anything and think about the goal again tomorrow.

Activity 5.9
Happy Memories

Notes

This activity helps the young person to recall happy memories. It is important to support them in understanding that happy memories are an important part of maintaining well-being.

Introduce the idea that they may find it helpful to think about happy memories when they are finding something tough; lots of people do this and find it helpful.

This is an activity during which the young person is invited to be as creative as they like, using a range of drawings, pictures, or other materials. Students may wish to create on a computer.

Worksheet 5.9
Happy Memories

Create your Happy Memories Picture in the frame below and include events, people and objects!

My Happy Memories

Activity 5.10
Reflective Writing

Notes

Written exercises that focus on sources of personal strength can help students learn the resilience-building strategies that work best for them as individuals.

For example, in exploring the answers to the questions on the worksheet that follows, students become more aware of their strengths and what they look for in supportive relationships with others.

Worksheet 5.10
Reflective Writing

1 Write about a person who supported you during a particularly stressful or traumatic time. How did they help you overcome this challenge? What did you learn about yourself?

2 Write about a friend that you supported as he or she went through a stressful event. What did you do that most helped your friend? What did you learn about yourself?

3 Write about a time in your life when you had to cope with a difficult situation. What helped and hindered you as you overcame this challenge? What learning did you take away that will help you in the future?

Activity 5.11
Self-Reflection Questions

This activity builds on the previous 'Reflective Writing' activity, and provides us with a structured approach to self-reflection.

Think about or discuss each question in turn, allowing plenty of time for reflection and expanding your answers.

Keep revisiting the questions you have already answered, asking yourself: **Could I be more positive about myself?** Another way of phrasing this is: **If I was being more positive about myself, what would I say in answer to the question?**

Things I do well

⟲ What activities do you do outside school? Sports? Hobbies?

⟲ Are you a member of any school clubs?

⟲ What is your best/favourite subject at school? Why?

⟲ Have you ever won a medal or a prize?

⟲ Do you help out at home? Do you cook, look after younger brothers or sisters, and so on?

⟲ Do you enjoy any sports?

⟲ Have you ever tried an unusual activity?

⟲ Do you like using the computer or playing games on a PlayStation? Are there any games or activities you are really good at?

⟲ Are you a neat and tidy person? Are you organised?

⟲ What do you want to do when you leave school?

Good times

☞ What is your favourite place?

☞ Where do you like to go with your friends/family?

☞ Where do you feel safest?

☞ Where do you go to relax?

☞ Have you a special moment in your life you can remember?

☞ Can you remember a school trip you particularly enjoyed?

☞ Have you ever been anywhere special on holiday?

☞ What do you like to do at weekends?

Personal characteristics

☞ How would the person that knows/loves you best describe you?

☞ What do your friends like about you?

☞ When was the last time you helped someone?

☞ Is there anyone you look after or help to look after?

☞ Have you any pets that you care for?

☞ What do you like best about yourself?

Activity 5.12
Three Good Things

We know that people who are grateful tend to be happier, healthier and more fulfilled. It may sound strange, but being grateful can help people to cope with stress. You may want to ask the young person why they think it is important to be grateful.

Introduce these ideas and emphasise that even on bad days there are good things that we can see and it is helpful to notice them, even if they are small.

This activity also provides a structure for helping young people to see that noticing positives can help them to rise to challenges, rather than dwelling on the negative in a situation.

Some young people will require support to engage in this activity and you can help them to think about everyday examples of 'good things', for example:

- I sat next to my friend at lunch.

- We had a PE lesson.

- I am reading a book I like.

- I played football at lunchtime.

In the session you will help them to practise, using the worksheet, by thinking about three good things that happened yesterday. You may want to use the school timetable to help the young person to remember the day and what they did and what might have been good.

Once the young person has completed this activity with you, provide them with additional worksheets so that they can try to use them on a daily basis for a week; they can then bring these along to your next session.

Worksheet 5.12
Three Good Things

Each day write down three good things that happened. They can be anything you feel good about or grateful for.

To get used to the idea, start by filling in the boxes below to describe three good things that happened to you **yesterday** and why they were good.

Remember! Even on a bad day there are normally some things that we can feel good about. Taking time to be grateful is not about ignoring the bad things – it just helps us focus our attention more on the positive, rather than dwelling on the negative.

Try to include **why** you felt each of the things was really good.

Good Thing 1
Good Thing 2
Good Thing 3

Now repeat this activity **at the end of each day** for a week. Use the blank boxes on the following pages to write down your Three Good Things each day.

My Good Things Diary

Good Thing 1

Why ...

Good Thing 2

Why ...

Good Thing 3

Why ...

Activity 5.13
Acts of Kindness

Doing things to help others is not only good for the recipients – it has a positive payback for our happiness and health too. When people experience kindness it also makes them kinder as a result – so kindness is contagious!

Put simply – **if you want to feel good, do good**.

Perform one extra act of kindness each day.

This could be offering a compliment, a helping hand, a hug, a gift, or something else. The act may be large or small and the recipient may not even be aware of it.

Ideally your acts of kindness should be beyond the kind things you already do on a regular basis. And of course the acts mustn't put you or others in danger!

Do at least one extra kind act each day for a week – ideally a **different** one each day.

Activity 5.14
Note of Thanks

Appreciate the good things about a person who is important to you.

Focus on one special person in your life and take time to think through the following questions – in each case try to note down specific examples:

1 What drew you to your special person when you first met?

_____

_____

_____

_____

2 What things have you really enjoyed doing together during your relationship?

_____

_____

_____

_____

3 What things do you really appreciate about them right now?

_____

_____

_____

_____

4 What are their strengths?

_____

_____

_____

_____

Then STOP AND OBSERVE AND NOTICE! When you're with that person, take the time to notice and acknowledge these things – their strengths, the things they do that you really appreciate, the happy times you've shared together, and so on.

I really love it when you ...
You're so good at ...
Seeing you do ... reminds me of that fantastic day when we ...

Things to consider

- It isn't always realistic to do this type of reflection for all of the people we know. But we can use the ideas to think about all of the positives in our relationships.

- An idea to try: before spending time with someone, take a moment just to think about the things you like and appreciate about them, what you admire about them, or how they make you feel good.

- Remember: after spending time with someone, think about the things you appreciated or what you enjoyed about your time together.

Now write that letter of thanks!

Activity 5.15
Stop & Savour

Savouring means .... any thoughts
or behaviours capable of 'generating,
intensifying and prolonging enjoyment'

Bryant & Veroff (2006)

To be able to savour positive
moments is an important part of
being happy and increasing our
well-being

(Seligman, 2003)

Questions for me!

What are your most enjoyable activities?

_____

How frequently do you STOP AND SAVOUR these experiences?

_____

How do you savour these activities?

_____

When do you savour these activities?

_____

What prevents you from savouring?

_____

Why do we sometimes just 'rush through' an activity, such as eating?

_____

Why do we not take the time to simply stop and take in our surroundings?

_____

Why do you think we have to make 'savouring' a deliberate act?

_____

Activity 5.16
Positive Events Calendar

Being in the moment and appreciating the good things that happen to us is extremely important. Keep a regular record of such events. Be aware of one pleasant event or occurrence each day *while* it is happening. This will build mindfulness and increase feelings of overall happiness and well-being. Record your experience in the worksheet.

Worksheet 5.16
Positive Events Calendar

	What was the experience?	Were you aware of the pleasant feelings while the event was happening?	How did your body feel, in detail, during this experience?	What moods, feelings and thoughts accompanied this event?	What thoughts are in your mind right now, as you write this down?
Monday					
Tuesday					
Wednesday					
Thursday					
Friday					
Saturday					
Sunday					

Activity 5.17
Take up the Challenge

My main challenge is:

Stage 1 — My steps to succeed are:

∽

∽

∽

∽

Stage 2 — What can I say to myself to help me?

page 1 of 2

Stage 3 — Visualise yourself being successful!

Repeat your coping self-talk (Stage 2) while you imagine taking the first step on Stage 1! Keep practising this!

Experiment!

Pick a time to face your fear or challenge – TRY IT OUT – take your first step and use your self-talk.

Stage 5 — Reward!

Treat yourself for being successful!

Don't give up! Keep going!

**Break the steps down into smaller ones
if you don't succeed at first!**

Activity 5.18
My Resilience Snake

On the outline of the snake, using the ups and downs of the shape, reflect on and write down past good and happy times and not so good, or difficult, times. (If you like, you can use key words that are meaningful only to you to keep details private.) Think about these times and consider the following questions.

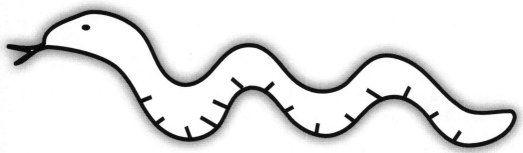

What helped you to bounce back after the difficult times?

_____

Did you feel any different after the difficult times?

_____

Did you gain anything from the difficulty?

_____

What did you learn?

_____

What was it about you that helped you through?

_____

What might you do differently?

_____

Are you aware of anyone else who has been through this difficult time?

_____

Activity 5.19
Top Tips for Developing Resilience

Resilience can be learnt. The following are some tips for helping you foster resilience. Which ones do you already use? Which others could you incorporate into your own personal strategy for fostering resilience? Tick the tips you think would be helpful and that you might try to use.

Self-care: In order to be resilient you need to take care of yourself in terms of your physical and mental health. Pay attention to your needs and feelings. Engage in activities that you enjoy and find relaxing. Exercise regularly and eat healthy food. This means that you will be ready for difficult situations when they arise.

Viewpoint: The way we view negative life events is important. Do you see your response as fixed and unchangeable or temporary and subject to influence?

Nothing lasts forever: When you are having a bad time, and are experience difficult feelings, it is important to acknowledge these feelings, remembering that they won't last, be kind to yourself knowing that all feelings (positive and negative) will pass.

Listen to your feelings: Learn to notice and listen to your emotions, be aware of what they are communicating so that you can accept them and manage your response. It is important to respond to your feelings, not fight them.

You are not alone: Recognise that you are not alone, and that others suffer in the same way. Difficulty is part of the human condition.

Reach out for help: Develop caring and supportive relationships – reach out for support. Talk to someone – friends, family, a teacher, a therapist. There is no shame in seeking help when you need it.

Learn from others: Observe role models – people who have coped with adversity – bearing in mind we are all different. Look at what has helped others.

Success stories: When reading stories or discussing events in the news it is useful to notice how people manage to overcome difficulties. Learn from other people's successes and strengths.

page 1 of 3

Empathise: Be curious about other people's perspectives as well as your own. When we empathise with others we feel less alone and less entrenched in pain, and as a result recover faster.

Seek solutions: Understand that where there is a problem there is a solution – even if it is not perfect, it can help the situation.

Get organised: Planning and problem solving can help us get through difficult times. Make changes where this is possible but recognise and accept things that you cannot change. For example, you cannot change how someone is behaving but you can change how you respond to them.

Be reflective: Writing about your thoughts or using the practice of meditation can also help.

Keep it in perspective: Without invalidating or ignoring the difficulty, try to keep it in perspective – problems are usually confined to one part of our lives, balance with what is going well in your life.

Learn from difficulty: Look for opportunities for self-discovery as a result of the difficulty. What have you learnt? What would you do differently?

Help others: If it is possible, redirect some of your energy away from your problems and towards helping others as this can help put your difficulties in perspective and also connect you to others and utilise your strengths, then boosting your confidence to manage your own difficulties.

Gratitude: Foster a habit of looking at all the good things around you. Keep a gratitude diary, regularly writing about things that are going well or that you are grateful for. For example: the loving people in your life, a beautiful spring day, your good health, your pets.

Positive places: Seek out positive environments – a beautiful park, a friendly club, places where you can feel calm, included or have a sense of belonging.

Have fun: Remember the value of humour – laughing can be a great release (but only if it is well intentioned).

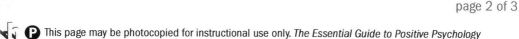

Optimism: Try visualising what you want an outcome to be rather than worrying about what you fear. Think about what your preferred future looks like. Perhaps draw it and think about steps to get there.

Strengths: Sustain a positive view of yourself and have confidence in your strengths and abilities – we all have them. Think back to previous times when you have managed difficult times, identify what was it about you that made it possible?

My Personal Resilience Strategy

Name: _____

I will aim to use the strategies I have ticked to foster and sustain my resilience.

Date: _____

Optional well-being development diary work

- ☞ Keep track of your resilience – a diary of your ups and downs, noting what you thought, felt and did.

- ☞ Also note what helped you to cope and what you would do differently in the future.

Activity 5.20
Effort & Outcome

This activity will help you to explore and consider the link between effort and outcome. The idea is that we are generally more motivated to do something when we think that our actions will result in an outcome that we want. The story of J.K. Rowling, the author of the Harry Potter books, provides an example of perseverance in difficult circumstances which results in a positive outcome.

Consider the story of J.K. Rowling, now on the most famous authors in the world, if not the most famous.

J.K. Rowling thought of the idea for a story of a young boy attending a school of wizardry when on a delayed train from Manchester to London. When she began writing Harry Potter, her mother died and she used these feelings to write about Harry's own feelings of loss in the first book. She continued to write the book on an old manual typewriter. Her marriage broke down and she became a single mother. She became depressed and had very little money. But still she continued to write. She submitted the manuscript to twelve different publishers who all rejected it. When she finally found someone to publish it, they told her that she should get a 'day job' because she was unlikely to make money out of the book. Her net worth has been estimated by some as $1.2 billion.

J.K. Rowling once told an audience of students, 'You might never fail on the scale I did but it is impossible to live without failing at something, unless you live so cautiously that you might as well not have lived at all – in which case you fail by default'.

In pairs, consider the following questions:

↪ What do you think of this story?

↪ What might have happened if she had given up?

↪ What do you think she meant by her quote?

↪ Can you think of an example of when you have put in a lot of effort and achieved something?

6 Activities for Groups

Activity 6.1
Group Agreement

Notes

With all group work it is crucial to identify an agreed set of rules for those working in the group. Establishing a group agreement allows the young people in the group and the facilitator to create a supportive, trusting and respectful environment from the start.

You may wish to act as a scribe for the group in this activity and record these ideas on flip chart paper or a whiteboard.

It is very important that the group members feel in control and empowered by the process of coming up with the rules they would like to agree on. It is extremely valuable to allow time for the group to come up with their own ideas, in their own words, and to discuss them in detail; this ensures that they develop a shared understanding and feel ownership of the group.

However, it can be helpful to have suggestions as a useful prompt if you feel that the group would benefit from more structure in the rule-making process.

A useful suggestion when facilitating this discussion is that the statements will be best if written as a positive declaration rather than a list of do's and don'ts.

Some suggestions follow, either for your own reference, or to be shared with the group:

↪ We will take turns to talk without interrupting.

↪ We will listen to each other and respect the views of everyone.

↪ We will encourage each other to speak up and make sure everyone can speak.

↪ We will be kind to each other/show understanding/show empathy for each other.

↪ We will respect each other.

↪ We will speak to each other with respect.

↪ We will respect each other's different beliefs and values.

↪ We will respect confidentiality – what we say in the room stays in the room.

↪ We can chose not to take part in any activity or conversation.

↪ We will all try to help each other.

You can record the group rules on the worksheet that follows, or a whiteboard. It may be helpful to ensure that each member of the group is provided with a copy to refer to in their own personal files.

Worksheet 6.1
Our Group Agreement

★ _____
_____

★ _____
_____

★ _____
_____

★ _____
_____

★ _____
_____

★ _____
_____

★ _____
_____

★ _____
_____

Activity 6.2
Well-being & Happiness

Notes

This activity involves discussing two important key words: happiness and well-being.

The group is separated into two, smaller groups.

1 One group will come up with as many ideas as possible to answer the question: 'What is happiness?'

2 The other group will come up with as many ideas as possible to answer the question: 'What is well-being?'

Allow about 10-15 minutes for this discussion. Then, ask the two groups to come together, share their ideas and discuss the similarities and differences they notice.

Ensure you facilitate the discussion of what is similar about these words, as well as what is different. Discuss the importance of an individual's own experience of well-being, rather than what is perceived by other people.

Activity 6.3a
Building Strengths 1

Seligman's 24 Character Strengths

These are the 24 character strengths described by psychologist Martin Seligman.

Look at each one and discuss it with a partner. Try to formulate a definition for each: you may need to look some up. What does each strength mean to you?

Creativity	Citizenship
Curiosity	Fairness
Open-mindedness	Leadership
Love of learning	Forgiveness
Keeping perspective	Humility
Bravery	Prudence
Persistence	Self-regulation
Integrity	Appreciation of beauty
Vitality	Gratitude
Love	Hope
Kindness	Humour
Social intelligence	Spirituality

Activity 6.3b
Building Strengths 2

Your group may decide to do this in the same session as Building Strengths 1, or at a later date.

Look at the words for the different strengths below. Cut them out individually. Then place them in order: first your greatest strengths, then your weakest. Take some time to reflect upon these.

Question 1: How can you further build upon your biggest strengths?

Question 2: Where/in which situations might you be able to use them in the future?

Creativity	Citizenship
Curiosity	Fairness
Open-mindedness	Leadership
Love of learning	Forgiveness
Keeping perspective	Humility
Bravery	Prudence
Persistence	Self-regulation
Integrity	Appreciation of beauty
Vitality	Gratitude
Love	Hope
Kindness	Humour
Social intelligence	Spirituality

Activity 6.4
Investigating Strengths

Notes

This activity can be used as a stand-alone activity, or it can be used to follow on from Activities 6.3a and 6.3b, 'Building Strengths 1 & 2'. It provides a structure for young people to assess their strengths and then focus on using these in new ways.

Worksheet 6.4
Investigating Strengths

Step 1: Identify your strengths

Carry out the VIA Character Strengths assessment here (takes up to 30 minutes):

www.authentichappiness.sas.upenn.edu/Tests/SameAnswers.

The assessment is called 'VIA Strength Survey for Children'. You will need to set up a log-in to use this site. https://www.authentichappiness.sas.upenn.edu/questionnaires/strength-survey-children

This shows which of 24 character strengths are your 'signature strengths'. Make sure you answer the questions on the assessment as you really are, not how you think you should be!

How do these results compare to your earlier assessment? What has changed?

Note down your **top five strengths** from the survey results:

Strength 1
Strength 2
Strength 3
Strength 4
Strength 5

Step 2: Review your strengths

Have a look at each of your top 5 in turn and ask yourself:

↻ Do you feel naturally drawn to this strength (excited, energised, etc.)?

↻ Do I feel surprised by it – is this the real me?

↻ How much do I use this strength currently (at work, at home, etc.)?

↻ Would others see it in me? (If you're not sure, ask them!)

If you don't feel that one of the five is the real you, then look at numbers 6, 7 or 8 and ask the same questions. Get to a list of 5 that you feel really are 'you'.

Step 3: Use your strengths

Pick one of your top 5 strengths and ask yourself:

↻ How do I use this already and in what areas of my life?

↻ What are other areas in my life that I could use it more?

↻ What are other ways I could use it?

Every day over the next week, try to use this strength in a new way or a new area of your life.

Repeat the following week, using another of your top 5. And so on ...

Based on work by Seligman M.E., Steen T.A., Park N. & Peterson C. (2005)

Activity 6.5
The Meaning of Happiness

During this activity, your group is going to discuss what happiness actually means, using a series of questions to guide you. Take your time and reflect carefully on how you feel about each question.

1 How important are these factors in being happy?

- Money

- Having power

- Being young

- Being important or famous

- Good health

- Interesting work

- Good friends

- Love

- Having a flashy car, a nice house

- Having children

2 Does happiness depend on factors like these?

3 Or does it depend on a person's attitude to life and other people?

4 Does happiness come to us by accident? In what ways can we make ourselves happy? Some people who are seriously ill appear to be happy all the time. How is that possible? Is it better not to think about being happy or unhappy?

page 1 of 2

5 What are the things in your daily life that constantly make you happy? How could you be happier than you are now?

6 Are these important factors in unhappiness?

☞ Being without love

☞ Having nothing to do

☞ Being ill

☞ Being lonely

☞ Hurting someone else

7 Who is the happiest person you know? Why are they happy?

8 Is it possible to be happy without other people? Would you be happy if you lived alone in a forest or desert? What can a lonely person, for example, someone who is separated from their partner by death or divorce, do to make their life happy?

9 Are men and women happy in different ways and for different reasons?

10 Why do some people have a feeling of guilt when they are very happy? Is it wrong or selfish to be happy?

11 Is it important to be happy?

Activity 6.6
My Happiness

Take a moment to think about what happiness **means** to you. Record whatever comes into your head.

What does happiness mean to you?

Now think about specific things that often make you happy. These could be activities, people, places or anything else that comes to mind.

What things make you happy?

Share this with someone else in the group and discuss.

Activity 6.7
What I Overcame & What I Learned

Notes

As a teacher or learning professional, share a personal story about a time you had to work hard to get better at something. In this story, highlight:

- Hard work

- Strategies

- Help from others

Here's an example below of a personal story to share with students:

When I was in Year 5, I remember struggling with adding negative numbers. I had a hard time understanding what a 'negative' even meant when talking about a number — how can you have less than nothing? I ended up going through many of the sums in the maths text book and continuing to get many of them wrong.

I was very shy when I was a child so I didn't ask my teacher many questions, as I just did not have the confidence to do that. My thought was that I had reached the 'peak' of my ability in maths, and that it was basically all going to be downhill from here.

I eventually asked my mum about this topic and she explained to me the basic concept of negative numbers. This helped me understand it a little, but it was still unclear to me. I then researched on the internet for some examples from real life to show what these mysterious numbers represented outside of some abstract universe. Some of them made sense and others didn't. I still didn't entirely get it and I was so anxious that I wanted to just give up (or continue hoping that negative numbers were not going to appear in my maths lessons ever again).

I started to dislike the subject simply because I couldn't understand it anymore. However, instead of entirely giving up, I eventually gathered the courage to ask my teacher for help as well. She explained it in a few different ways and gave me new strategies to try out. After some practise with these new strategies, I started to solidify my understanding of negatives, which allowed me to quickly pick up basic algebra afterwards. While it was a lot of hard work and I wanted to give up at many points during my journey, I eventually was able to 'rewire' my brain so that negative numbers actually made sense to me.

In small groups, ask the group members to share a story about a time that they made their brains smarter.

Once these stories have been shared, move the discussion on to the themes of working hard, taking on challenges, and finding the right strategy that can make people smarter.

Activity 6.8
A Letter to a Future Student

This activity involves asking students to write a letter about a learning-related struggle that they have experienced. Ask them to consider the following:

- How did it make them feel?
- How did they overcome it?
- What did it teach them?

Ask them to write a letter to a future student to tell them about their struggle, what they learned from it, and any advice they could give to the other student. Collect their letters and save them in order to give them back to them during difficult testing periods, such as final exams.

Additional Activity

This activity looks at neuroplasticity and builds on the work done in the 'letter' activity above.

Ask the students to create a poster, painting, video, PowerPoint presentation, or simple computer programme to show how the brain works.

Ask them to answer these questions:

- What is neuroplasticity and how does it work?
- What are neurons? How can they change over time? How do we know this?
- What are ways of making your brain grow?
- What is a growth mind-set?

Encourage your students to be creative and scientific when explaining how learning can help develop the brain. If possible, allow them to research for themselves.

Display these projects around your classroom or the school corridors, and refer to them throughout the year to motivate and offer a friendly reminder about the brain's plasticity.

Activity 6.9
Hero Stories

This activity can involve short pieces of writing or group discussion exercises. The focus is on heroic characters as a way to reflect on resilience and the role it plays in life. It can be particularly useful to use with younger children.

After the children or young people have read a book or heard a story that features a heroic character, encourage them to reflect by answering the following questions:

- Who was the hero in this story? Why?

- What challenge or dilemma did the hero overcome?

- What personal strengths did the hero possess? What choices did they have to make?

- How did other people support the hero?

- What did the hero learn?

- How do we use the same personal strengths when we overcome obstacles in our own lives? Can you share some examples?

Activity 6.10
True or False?

Consider each of the following statements and discuss them in your group. Do you think they are true or false? Explain why you made each choice.

Money always makes people happy.	Having enough money to satisfy basic needs is important.
Wanting more and more money can make you feel depressed.	Living what you preach is more important than being rich.
Having good relationships makes you happier than having money.	Using money to help others will make you happy.
Materialistic people are less happy than people who aren't worried about possessions.	People who are well off generally experience good health.
An increase in income ensures an increase in well-being.	Working to achieve goals makes you happier than actually reaching them

Activity 6.11
Self-Reflection Questions

Go through the following questions individually. At the end of the session you'll have a chance to share with another group member and discuss your responses.

As you work through the questions, keep revisiting them and ask yourself: **Could I be more positive about myself?** Another way of phrasing this question is: **If I was being more positive about myself what would I say?**

Things I do well

↪ What activities do you do outside school? Sports? Hobbies?

↪ Are you a member of any school clubs?

↪ What is your best/favourite subject at school? Why?

↪ Have you ever won a medal or a prize?

↪ Do you help out at home? Do you cook, look after younger brothers or sisters, and so on?

↪ Do you enjoy any sports?

↪ Have you ever tried an unusual activity?

↪ Do you like using the computer or playing games on a PlayStation? Are there any games or activities you are really good at?

↪ Are you a neat and tidy person? Are you organised?

↪ What do you want to do when you leave school?

Good times

↪ What is your favourite place?

↪ Where do you like to go with your friends/family?

↪ Where do you feel safest?

↪ Where do you go to relax?

↪ Have you a special moment in your life you can remember?

↪ Can you remember a school trip you particularly enjoyed?

↪ Have you ever been anywhere special on holiday?

↪ What do you like to do at weekends?

Personal characteristics

↪ How would the person that knows/loves you best describe you?

↪ What do your friends like about you?

↪ When was the last time you helped someone?

↪ Is there anyone you look after or help to look after?

↪ Have you any pets that you care for?

↪ What do you like best about yourself?

Work through the questions, taking your time.

Then share your responses with someone else in the group.

Could you be more positive about yourself?

Activity 6.12
Stop & Savour

✍ Get into pairs

✍ Discuss the two statements below about 'savouring'

✍ Ask each other the questions listed below

> Savouring means .... any thoughts or behaviours capable of 'generating, intensifying and prolonging enjoyment'
>
> Bryant & Veroff (2006)

> To be able to savour positive moments is an important part of being happy and increasing our well-being
>
> (Seligman, 2003)

Questions for me!

What are your most enjoyable activities?

_____

How frequently do you STOP AND SAVOUR these experiences?

_____

How do you savour these activities?

_____

When do you savour these activities?

_____

What prevents you from savouring?

_____

Why do we sometimes just 'rush through' an activity, such as eating?

_____

Why do we not take the time to simply stop and take in our surroundings?

_____

Why do you think we have to make 'savouring' a deliberate act?

_____

Activity 6.13
Compliments Cards

Ask the group what they feel about the importance of giving compliments:

↪ Why is it good to give compliments?

↪ What do we usually compliment in other people?

↪ What does it feel like to get a compliment?

Using the worksheet that follows, ask everyone to write compliment cards to give to those they want to compliment. You may want to consider modelling this compliment activity by writing compliment cards to give to each member of the group at the start of the session to introduce the key ideas.

Optional

Another consideration for this group activity is to suggest that the group may want to write compliment cards to another member of the group. Careful consideration should be given to this in advance, and you should only think about doing this if you feel confident that the group has positive dynamics that would embrace participation by all members.

If you suggest that compliments cards are written for group members, it is important to ensure that each member of the group receives a compliment card. You may need to structure this part of the activity to ensure this, for example: the group may write compliments to each other in pairs, or they may all sit in a circle and write compliments to the person on their right. This activity should only be done if you are confident the group can engage in a way that will be positive for all members.

Worksheet 6.13
Compliments Cards

Send a private compliment using the postcards below.

Activity 6.14
Gratitude Attitude

Have a gratitude attitude!

What are you grateful for?

Take a moment and really think.

Think of something you are grateful for:

> And another thing …
>
> And another thing …
>
> And another thing …

I am grateful for …

_____

_____

_____

_____

When we start to think about what we are grateful for it makes us feel good!	Every day can be gratitude day!

Activity 6.15
How Assertive Am I? A Quiz

Everyone in the group can have a go at completing this quiz and then discuss/feedback in the group

Score each statement from 1 to 5

	Always	1	2	3	4	5	Never	

1 I often agree with others to avoid feelings of guilt/anxiety _____

2 I am uncomfortable offering my thoughts in class/a group where no one else agrees with me _____

3 I struggle to tell others when they are making me uncomfortable _____

4 I would avoid asking someone to return something they had borrowed from me _____

5 I find it difficult to return faulty goods to a shop _____

6 I avoid asking others to help complete tasks, I will usually just keep going myself _____

7 I would avoid correcting someone who has mispronounced my name, even if they continue to do it _____

8 I would not usually volunteer or offer to go first _____

9 I wouldn't be able to just talk with a complete stranger _____

10 I struggle to say no to others without apologising _____

11 I tend not to treat myself _____

12 I am unlikely to make the first move to ask someone out _____

13 Other people's views tend to be better than mine _____

14 I usually get in trouble because of other people _____

page 1 of 2

15 Often my social group will do things that I don't enjoy ⎯⎯

16 I don't usually like to make too much of a fuss about anything ⎯⎯

17 I deserve to be unfairly treated ⎯⎯

18 Once I've said yes, I can't really change my mind ⎯⎯

19 Others often get away with saying unkind things to me/making me look or feel studid ⎯⎯

20 I would be unlikely to challenge someone who cuts in front me in a lunch queue/line ⎯⎯

Scoring

Add your total score and use the key below to help you reflect on your responses.

Key

80+ You appear to have a consistently assertive approach; chances are you handle most situations well enough. Keep it up!

60-79 You're somewhat assertive. Chances are there will be some situations that you can handle better than others. Keep practising; you'll get better over time!

40-59 You have some assertive qualities but you're more inclined to respond either passively or aggressively. It might be useful for you to take some time to think about your perception of situations, then rehearse and practise some of the top tips for assertiveness!

20-39 You struggle to be assertive. You need to take time to think about your perceptions understanding of situations. It will be really useful for you to think about the top tips for assertiveness and take some time to rehearse and practise!

Activity 6.16
Acceptance Cards — It's Good to Be You!

Cut out the cards and play the Acceptance Game.

Work in groups of 6 to 8 people. Nominate one person to shuffle the cards and then start by taking the top card and completing the sentence or answering the question. Return the card to the bottom of the pile and then continue around the group until all the cards have been used. You can take another card or pass if necessary.

Worksheet 6.16
Acceptance Cards — It's Good to Be You!

I'm good at ...	Say two things you like about the person opposite.	I know I'm successful when ...
I'm getting better at ...	I know when others accept me because ...	My best point is ...
My main strengths are ...	My mum or dad or carer thinks I'm good at ...	My best day was ...
I think my friends like me because ...	I know that my mum or dad or carer accepts me for who I am because ...	My friends like me because ...
I like myself because ...	I feel positive when ...	My best subject is ...
I care a lot about ...	If you could be anyone else in the group who would it be and why?	The best bit about how I look is ...
What is most important to me is ...	It's Good to be You!	My greatest talent is ...
I feel important when ...	Tell the person opposite what people like about him or her.	I know I have the power to ...
My best achievement is ...	In this game I most respect [person's name] because ...	My best quality is ...
Turn to the person on your right and identify two positive things about them.	I feel confident when ...	Turn to the person on your left and identify two positive things about them.

Activity 6.17
Self–Acceptance Checklist

Rate yourself against each of the following statements on a scale of 1 to 10 (1=not at all, 5=a medium amount, 10=totally).

How do you need to develop/improve your levels of self-acceptance and self-esteem?

Discuss with a partner and feedback to the group.

People who accept themselves and have good self-esteem:

- Have certain values they believe in, act on and can defend. At the same time they are secure enough to alter these, if they need to.

- Are able to act in their own best interests without excessive guilt. If they make 'mistakes' they are able to accept this and learn.

- Value themselves and see themselves as being of value to others, particularly to those with whom they associate.

- Are sensitive to the needs and feelings of others.

- View others positively, looking for the best in them.

- Remain confident in their ability to deal with problems, even when things seem to be gong badly.

- Feel equal to others as a person – not superior or inferior – irrespective of the differences in abilities, backgrounds or attitudes.

- Accept praise without false modesty or rejection.

- Resist the efforts of others to dominate them or put them down.

- Accept the range of desires and feelings they experience – positive and negative. It does not follow from this that they will act on all desires and feelings.

- Do not worry unduly about the future or past.

Activity 6.18
Positive Memories

Remembering past events, situations or people with love and affection and in a positive way is a very important way of maintaining our well-being. It is particularly useful to develop the ability to transport yourself to positive past times when times get tough or challenging.

Create your Positive Memories Collage in the space below and include events, people and objects! Discuss in your group and see what you have in common.

My Positive Memories Collage

Activity 6.19
The Best Me

This is a timed writing activity. Think about what would be your best possible future self in all areas of your life – including home, school, career, friends, family etc. Then take 20 minutes to record your ideas on the diagram below.

Repeat this exercise on a daily basis for one week and then consider the impact upon your happiness levels. Share your findings in the group!

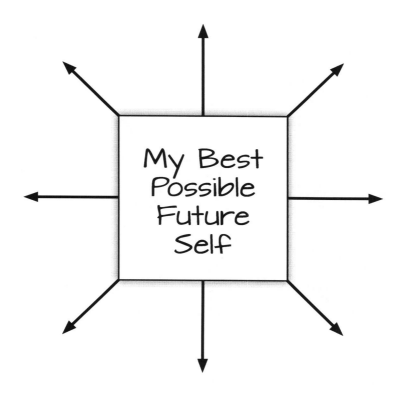

Activity 6.20
Top Talk — Helping Others

When you keep experiencing the same problem, it can really help to find someone else who copes with the same issues. Talk through their strategies and the steps they have taken towards success.

Answer the following questions:

☞ What is this problem?

_____

_____

_____

☞ Who has successfully coped with this problem?

_____

_____

_____

☞ How do they do this?

_____

_____

_____

☞ When can I discuss their plan?

_____

_____

_____

☞ What will my own plan then look like and when will I try it out?

_____

_____

_____

☞ How will I reward myself for being successful?

_____

_____

_____

Resources

Handouts

1 Information Sheet & Consent Form for Parents & Carers
2 Top Tips for Teens Dealing with Stress & Anxiety
3 Assertiveness & Confidence – Information Sheet for Young People
4 Strategies that Might Develop Confidence & Assertiveness
5 Information Sheet for Young People/Parents/Carers - Resilience

References

Information Sheet & Consent Form for Parents & Carers

Positive Psychology

There is an increasing amount of research that suggests that young people today may experience a range of challenges, from low self-esteem and anxiety to other emotional difficulties. The well-being of our students is a priority of our school and this is why we provide support at both an individual and whole-school level to ensure that all our students can develop and maintain good mental health.

What is Positive Psychology?

This is an approach which is based on looking to increase what is going well, rather than trying to 'fix' what is wrong. Positive Psychology identifies and explores strengths and weaknesses and looks to build on strengths to support overall emotional well-being.

How will my child benefit?

Research shows us that Positive Psychology interventions can make a difference in a wide range of areas including: reducing negative emotions, building resilience, supporting positive progress for those experiencing depression and other mental health issues.

What should I do if I have any further questions about the programme?

Please contact _____
if you have any further questions or concerns.

Consent & Permissions

I agree to let my child participate in the sessions.

I understand that I can withdraw my child from the session at any time and do not have to state a reason.

Signed _____ (parent/carer)

Print name _____ Date _____

Top Tips for Teens Dealing with Stress & Anxiety

Stress is a feeling of mental strain that can affect your well-being.

A stressor is anything that causes stress, for example, exams.

Anxiety is an unhelpful feeling of intense fear that affects your well-being.

A phobia is an intense fear of something that poses little or no actual danger.

A panic attack is a rush of intense anxiety with physical symptoms, for example, shortness of breath.

Remember: A bit of stress can help you do things (e.g., try something new), but too much can be bad for your well-being. You are the best person to notice what 'too much' is.

↪ Try to identify your stressors. Sometimes keeping a journal can help you do this.

↪ Try to identify what it feels like when you are stressed. Draw or write it down.

↪ Try to identify what calms you down and makes you feel good – plan it into your daily life.

↪ Think about sharing this knowledge with friends, family, teachers.

↪ Remember that lots of people feel stressed and anxious, and that stress and anxiety can both be managed and treated. Don't suffer in silence; think about who you could talk to or where you could go for help.

↪ Here are a few places that might be helpful to find out more:

○ http://www.youngminds.org.uk/for_children_young_people/better_mental_health

○ https://www.apa.org/helpcenter/stress-teens.aspx

○ http://kidshealth.org/en/teens/stress.html

page 1 of 2

A few stress busting ideas to consider:

- ↻ Plan in some exercise

- ↻ Spend time with people who make you feel good

- ↻ Write or draw a journal

- ↻ Spend time with pets

- ↻ Get a mindfulness app on your phone and build some meditation into your day

- ↻ Join a yoga class

- ↻ Recognise the rituals and routines that make you feel good

- ↻ Keep a gratitude diary – write down one thing each day that you are grateful for, however small

- ↻ Do some small acts of kindness

- ↻ Write a list of things you are good at

- ↻ Get a friend or family member to write a list of things you are good at

- ↻ Watch a film

- ↻ Listen to music

- ↻ Grow something

- ↻ Play

- ↻ Volunteer

- ↻ Write a letter

Assertiveness & Confidence — Information Sheet for Young People

Confidence and assertiveness are essential life skills. The development of these skills will help to keep our emotional and mental health and well-being in good shape. They will also help us to build positive relationships with others.

Some key definitions:

Confidence: The feeling or belief that someone can have faith in or rely on someone or something.

Assertiveness: Having or showing a confident or forceful personality.

The main differences between the two: Confidence is the feeling; it is the internal interaction with anything we go through. Assertiveness is the behaviour, we can be confident without being assertive.

The Pitfalls of a Lack of Confidence or Assertiveness

A lack of confidence and assertiveness can affect many areas of our lives, including:

- Relationships
- Bullying
- Victim Mentality/Learned Helplessness

Relationships

With respect to friendships, a person who lacks confidence and who is not assertive could tend to go with the crowd and take part in activities that they might not be comfortable with. Often, going with the majority is not too much of an issue – for example, a group picking a film to watch at the cinema or choosing where to have lunch.

> *'I've got great friends, why is this a problem?'*

A lack of confidence can become problematic when friendship groups are choosing activities which might matter more than where to have lunch – for instance going to parties/bars/clubs, friends choosing to drink/smoke/take drugs together, or maybe even going along with a popular crowd who bully others.

page 1 of 2

Bullying

If we think about someone who is not very assertive, how might this mean that they are likely to be bullied or targeted in certain settings?

Bullying can take the form of what we typically regard as bullying behaviour, for example, physical or verbal intimidation.

It can also take the form of such things as subtle comments: 'You're not really good enough to compete at this level' or 'I wouldn't bother if I were you' or 'That was good enough for a boy or girl'.

Bullying can also take the form of being 'short-changed' (e.g., asking for a small drink in a shop, being given a large instead and then being expected to pay for the large drink or being overcharged for an item in a shop).

It can also affect how a person reacts to or deals with inappropriate behaviour in public (e.g., a person is invading your personal space and/or tries to touch you on a train or someone sitting in a seat that you had paid to reserved in the cinema).

Over time, if this is a common occurrence we might start to develop a victim mentality or 'play the victim'. This means that we start to internalise these responses, and our expectation is that bad things happen to us and we should just accept it. This is **dangerous**!

Victim Mentality/Learned Helplessness

A condition in which a person suffers from a sense of powerlessness, arising from a traumatic event, persistent failure to succeed or persistent negative responses. Learned helplessness can have long-term and pathological impacts, such as leading to depression.

Not being assertive enough and being involved in romantic relationships do not mix well, especially if we consider the idea of consent. This can include anything from being told what to wear, who to associate with or which friends to have, right through to being forced to send inappropriate pictures, take part in sexual activities, having sex, and the use of condoms.

REMEMBER

↪ You ALWAYS having a choice!

↪ Be sure to be comfortable with your decisions!

↪ You ARE allowed to change your mind!

Strategies that Might Develop Confidence & Assertiveness

Confidence

↪ Mindset – confidence is not a set of rules to follow, confidence is a state of being. Take a deep breath and a first step.

↪ Practise makes perfect – 'I fear not the man who has practised 10,000 kicks once, but I fear the man who has practised one kick 10,000 times' (Bruce Lee).

↪ Think about your surroundings – are the people around you good for your confidence? Are your surroundings conducive to thinking or feeling confident?

↪ 'Fake it till you make it' – part of 'faking it' is about convincing yourself things will work out the way you want them to. What's the worse that can happen?

↪ Preparation – think through things, plan out your steps and potential responses. It's better to be over-prepared than under-prepared.

↪ Think about past achievements – what things have you done already, how can you use them to push you forward? What value do they show?

↪ Think about your strengths – everyone has strengths, what are yours? How can you identify or use them?

↪ Prioritising – what is important to you? Manage your expectations and be realistic about what you want to achieve.

↪ Language – how do you refer to yourself? How do others refer to you? Is it in a positive way?

↪ Extraneous factors – how are things in your life right now? Are external factors (sleep, diet, other stress) having an impact on your confidence?

Assertiveness

- ↻ Balance – be honest and open about what you want but be prepared that things might not necessarily go the way you want them to.

- ↻ Timing – think about the impact, and necessity too, of being assertive at different times.

- ↻ It's all about choice – you **always** have a choice. Your choices have consequences. Think them through!

- ↻ Plan and practise – think things through, rehearse!

- ↻ Perspective – you are not rejecting a person, you are opposing an act/task/issue!

- ↻ Saying 'No' – you have the right to say no, learn to exercise it!

- ↻ Changing your mind – you have the change your mind; feel free to exercise it!

- ↻ Responsibility – yours is the only adult behaviour that you are responsible for!

- ↻ Processing – you have the right to think it over; do not be forced into making decisions!

- ↻ Knowledge – know your rights/opinions/wants/desires, this will make them easier to share with others.

- ↻ Self-worth – understand that you and your opinions have value!

- ↻ Implementation – every marathon starts with a first step.

- ↻ Presence – think about your eye-contact and the volume of your voice, more eye-contact with a higher volume is more likely to get you heard.

HANDOUT 5 Information Sheet for Young People/Parents/Carers

What is Resilience?

Definitions:

↪ Resilience is the capacity to recover from difficulty.

↪ Resilience is our ability to adapt and bounce back when things do not go as planned.

↪ Resilience is the process of adapting well in the face of adversity, trauma, tragedy, threats or significant sources of stress.

↪ Being resilient does not mean that a person does not experience difficulty and distress. Emotional pain and sadness are common in people who have suffered major adversity or trauma. The road to recovery is likely to involve emotional distress.

↪ Resilience is not a trait that people either have or do not have. It involves behaviours, thoughts and actions that can be learned and developed in anyone.

Resilience is not an all or nothing concept/trait. It comes in amounts. You can be a little resilient or a lot of resilient; resilient in some situations and but others. No matter how resilient someone is today, they can become more resilient tomorrow. We learn from our difficulties.

Quick resilience quiz:

You can use the link below to carry out a quick resilience test.

http://resiliencyquiz.com/index.shtml

References

Ankeny E. & Lehmann J., 2011, 'Journey Towards Self-Determination: Voices of students with disabilities who participated in secondary transition program on community college campus', *Remedial and Special Education* 32(4), pp279–289.

Barnes J. (ed.), 1984, *The Complete Works of Aristotle*, vols 1–2, Princeton University Press, Princeton, NJ.

Baumeister R.F., 2005, *The Cultural Animal: Human nature, and social life, meaning*, Oxford University Press, Oxford.

Bryant F.B. & Veroff J., 2006, *Savoring: A New Model of Positive Experience*, Lawrence Erlbaum Associates Mahwah, NJ.

Buettner D., 2015, *The Blue Zones Solutions. Key takeaway, analysis and review*, Eureka Books, ePub.

Clifton D.O. & Anderson C.E., 2002, *Now Discover Your Strengths: How to develop your strengths and those of people like you*, Pocket Books, London.

Clifton O.D. & Rath T. 2004, *How full is your bucket? Positive strategies for work and life*, Gallup Press, New York .

Christakis N.A. & Fowler J.H., 2012, 'Social Contagion Theory: Examining dynamic social networks and human behaviour', *Statistics in Medicine* 32(4), pp556–77.

Csikszentmihalyi M., 2003, 'Legs or Wings? A reply to R. S. Lazarus', *Psychological Inquiry* 14, pp113–15.

Cummings R., Maddux C.D. & Casey J., 2000, 'Individualized Transition Planning for Students with Learning Disabilities', *Career Development Quarterly* 49 (1), pp60-72.

Dawood R., 2013, 'Positive Psychology in School-Based Psychological Intervention: A study of the evidence-base,' *The European Journal of Social & Behavioural Sciences* 113, pp44–53.

Dean J., 2013, *Making Habits, Breaking Habits: How to make changes that stick*, OneWorld Publications, London.

Deci E.L. & Vansteenkiste M., 2004, 'Self-Determination Theory and Basic Need Satisfaction: Understanding human development in positive psychology', *Ricerche di Psichologia 27*, pp17-34.

Donaldson S.I., Dollweta A. & Raoa M.A., 2014, 'Happiness, Excellence, and Optimal Human Functioning Revisited: Examining the peer-reviewed literature linked to positive psychology', *The Journal of Positive Psychology* 22(5), pp85-195.

Duckworth A. & Seligman M., 2005, 'Self- Discipline Outdoes IQ in Predicting Academic Performance of Adolescents', *Psychological Science* 16, pp939–44.

Duhigg C., 2012, *The Power of Habit: Why we do what we do and how to change*, Random House Books, London.

Dutton J., 2003, *Energize Your Workplace: How to create and sustain high-quality connections at work*, Jossey Bass, San Francisco.

Dweck C.S., 2006, *Mindset: The new psychology of success*, Ballantine Books, New York.

Fox Eades J.M., 2008, *Celebrating Strengths: Building strengths-based schools*, CAPP Press, Coventry.

Frederickson B., 2009, *Positivity*, Crown Publishers, New York.

Gable S.L., Reis H.T., Impett E. & Asher E.R., 2004, 'What Do You Do When Things Go Right? The intrapersonal and interpersonal benefits of sharing positive events', *Journal of Personality and Social Psychology* 87, pp228–45.

Gailliot M. & Baumeister R., 2006, 'Self-Regulation and Personality: How Interventions Increase Regulatory Success, and How Depletion Moderates the Effects of Traits on Behavior' *Journal of Personality*, 74:6, pp1773-1801.

Gardner H., 2011, *Frames of Mind: The theory of multiple intelligences*, 10th edn, Basic Books, Philadelphia.

Goleman D., 2007, *Social Intelligence: The new science of human relationships*, Arrow Books, London.

Howell A.J., 2009, 'Flourishing: Achievement-related correlates of students' well-being', *The Journal of Positive Psychology*, 4(1) p1-13.

Huebner E. S. & Hills K. J., 2011, 'Does the Positive Psychology Movement Have Legs for Children in Schools?', *The Journal of Positive Psychology* 6(1), pp88–94.

James W., *Habit*, 2018, Forgotten Books, London.

Kaufman S.B., 2014, *Ungifted: Intelligence Redefined. The truth about talent, practice, creativity, and the many paths to greatness*, Basic Books, New York.

Kraemer S., 1999, 'Promoting Resilience: changing concepts of parenting and child care', *International Journal of Child and Family Welfare*, 3, pp273-87.

Linley A., 2008, *Average to A+; Realizing strengths in yourself and others*, CAPP Press, Coventry.

MacConville R.M. & Rae T., 2012, *Building Happiness, Resilience and Motivation in Adolescents: A positive psychology curriculum for well-being*, Jessica Kingsley Publishers, London.

Maslow A.,1943, 'A theory of human motivation', *Psychological Review*, 50, pp370-96.

Michalec B., Diefenbeck C. & Mahoney M., 2013, 'The calm before the storm? Burnout and compassion fatigue among undergraduate students', *Nurse Educ. Today* 33, pp314–20.

Mischel W., 1966, 'Theory and research on the antecedents of self-imposed delay of reward', in B.A. Maher *Progress in Experimental Personality Research*, New York, Academic Press. pp. 85–131

Nettle D., 2005, *Happiness: The science behind your smile*, Open University Press, Oxford.

Peterson C. & Seligman M., 2004, *Character Strengths and Virtues: A handbook and Classification*, Oxford University Press, New York.

Roberts E., Ju S. & Zhang D., 2014, 'Review of Practices that Promote Self-advocacy for Students with Disabilities', *Journal of Disability Policy Studies*, 26(4) p209-20.

Rogers C., 1961, *On Becoming a Person: A Therapist's View of Psychotherapy*, Constable, London.

Ryan R.M. & Deci E.L., 2000, 'Self-determination Theory and the Facilitation of Intrinsic Motivation, Social Development, and Well-being', *American Psychologist* 55(1), pp68–78.

Seldon A., 2011, 'Today, Class, We Shall Build Your Character: Think Tank, new ideas for the 21st century', *The Times*, 31.11.11.

Seligman M.E.P., 2011, *Flourish: A visionary new understanding of happiness and well-being and how to achieve them*, Nicholas Brealey Publishing, London.

Seligman M.E.P., 2003, *Authentic Happiness: Using the new positive psychology to realize your potential for lasting fulfilment*, Free Press, New York.

Seligman M.E.P, 2002, 'Positive Psychology, Positive Prevention, and Positive Therapy', in Snyder C.R. & Lopez S.J. (eds), *Handbook of Positive Psychology*, pp3–9, Oxford University Press, New York.

Seligman M.E.P., Steen T.A., Park N. & Peterson C., 2005, '', *Am Psychol.* 60(5), pp410-21.

Seligman M.E.P. & Royzman E., 2003, https://www.authentichappiness.sas.upenn.edu/newsletters/authentichappiness/happiness

Seligman M.E.P. & Csikszentmihalyi M., 2000, 'Positive Psychology: An introduction', *American Psychologist* 55, pp5–14.

Smith I.K., 2010, *Happy: Simple steps to get the most out of life*, St. Martin's Press, New York.

Stiglbauer B., Gnambs T., Gamsjager M. & Batinic B., 2013, 'The Upward Spiral of Adolescents' Positive School Experiences and Happiness: Investigating reciprocal effects over time', *Journal of School Psychology* 51(2), pp231–42.

Suldo S.M. & Shaffer E.J., 2008, 'Looking Beyond Psychopathology: The dual-factor model of mental health in youth', *School Psychology Review* 37, pp52–68.

Syvertsen A.K., Roehlkepartain E.C., & Scales P.C., 2012, 'The American Family Assets Study', https://rhyclearinghouse.acf. hhs.gov/library/2012/key-findings-american-family-assets-study

Test D.W., Fowler C.H., Wood W.M., Brewer D.M. & Eddy S., 2005, 'A Conceptual Framework of Self-Advocacy for Students with Disabilities', *Remedial and Special Education* 26(1), pp43–54.

Tough P., 2012, *How Children Succeed: Grit, curiosity, and the hidden power of character*, Houghton Mifflin Harcourt, Boston.

Ungar M., 2006, *Strengths-Based Counselling with At-risk Youth*, Corwin Press, California.

Vaish A., Grossmann T. & Woodward A., 2008, 'Not All Emotions are Created Equal: The negativity bias in social-emotional development', *Psychological Bulletin* 134(3), pp383–403. http://doi.org/10.1037/0033-2909.134.3.383.

Wilson T.D., 2011, *Redirect: The surprising new science of psychological change*, Allen Lane, London.

Yeager J.M., Fisher S.W. & Shearon D.N., 2011, *Smart Strengths: Building character, resilience and relationships in youth*, Kravis Publishing, New York.